GREEK HEROES BEFORE AND DURING
THE WAR OF INDEPENDENCE:

ZAHARIAS, NIKOLOPOULOS & BARBITSIOTIS

BY

ANDREW PAGONIS

LIBRARY OF CONGRESS CAT. NUM. IN PUBLICATION DATA

ISBN: 1-885778-66-X

For additional information, please write to Seaburn Books
PO Box 2085
Long Island City, New York 11102
www.seaburn.com

"Greek Heroes Before and During the War of Independence: Zaharias, Nikolopoulos and Barbitsiotis," is about three heroes who played a pivotal role in their respected era's for Greece to achieve her freedom after nearly four centuries of slavery under the Ottoman Empire. The heroes are named, Zaharias (the) Barbitsiotis, Andonis Nikolopoulos and Petros Anagnostopoulos-Barbitsiotis and they all played a significant role in Greek society, by either laying the foundation for Greek Independence, or by continuing and preventing the Greek cause for liberation from becoming extinct. The book covers their life history and focuses on some of their major life events, which changed the history of Modern Greece. It also informs the readers about the major battles they faced their various ordeals they went through and a brief background about their family lineage. Also, the book includes information on the respected villages they came from and were based at. In addition, the book explains the close association and relationship between the three heroes and their home villages. It should also be mentioned that the book rightfully covers the social and government structure, along with the events in the Peloponnese leading up to the time period of when these three heroes started their glorious history.

Lately, there has been some focus and attention given to these three heroes, especially on Kapetan Zaharias. But more recognition is needed, which would shed a greater light on their accomplishments and their history. I have decided to write a book in English to inform the Greek Diaspora of the history of Zaharias, Nikolopoulos and Barbitsiotis, since very few people know anything about these heroes or even about the time period of the late 18th century to early 19th century Greece. Also, it is estimated that 67% of the Greek Diaspora does not read or understand Greek fully. Therefore, it is imperative to educate and foster this particular period of Greek history (since Ancient Greek is taught in the schools), which has shaped and influenced the modern Greek nation, so as to make the Greek Diaspora more aware of their heritage and inform the non-Greeks as well. Zaharias, Nikolopoulos and Barbitsiotis were great fighters, brilliant leaders, who possessed courage, strength, and a golden heart, and above all they were unselfish and patriotic. They had qualities, which every Greek, or individual for that matter, should follow and set an example.

Andrew Pagonis

I like to thank Takis Nikolopoulos for supplying me with some information on Andonis Nikolopoulos and Logastra from his personal archive.

PREFACE

Practically the entire world has heard of or has some knowledge of Greek heroes especially the ones who lived during antiquity. But Greece has also had its share of heroes during the modern era, which unfortunately the Greeks living in their native land, and the Diaspora (the so-called Greek Omogenia) have done very little or nothing at all to honor and pay tribute to these heroes. And if they have done something, whether by holding an annual ceremony, unveiling a statue, or conducting a memorial service for a hero, its only been for a small number of them. This is why the rest of the world has not heard much of anything about the heroes of modern Greece. Maybe if the Greek community would consider honoring and paying tribute to these heroes with various methods the rest of the world would catch on. In addition, the Greek community would be educating their children and future generations in keeping touch with their Greek roots, identity, culture and history.

The scope of this book is to shed some light on three Greek heroes who paved the way for the freedom of Greece from the Turkish Ottoman Empire and who played a major role in the Greek War of Independence. The three heroes in question are none other than Kapetan Zaharias Barbitsiotis, Kapetan Antonis Nikolopoulos, and Kapetan Petros Anagnostopoulos – Barbitsiotis. All three started out as Greek klephtes (rebels) who fought against the Turkish tyranny and the word "Kapetan:" in front of their names has its roots from the word "Captain." These men became commanders of their own rebel or klephtic unit, in which case they attained the title of "Kapetan."

The three men mentioned above lived in the same region of Greece, Laconia, and lived around the same time from the twilight years of the Turkish occupation of Greece to the war of independence. Out of the three heroes, Kapetan Zaharias made the biggest impact and changed the history of Modern Greece. He paved the road and build the foundation for Greek Independence. In order to this, he had to change the structure, the purpose and the thinking of the Greek klephtic rebels. One of his biggest accomplishments was the formation of the klephto-armatoloi federation of the Peloponnese, in which he became Commander in Chief, for the purpose of freeing Greece from the Turkish yoke. Unfortunately, he was assassinated about 17 years before the start of the Greek War of Independence. Had he lived, the war for independence would of started a lot sooner, since he was preparing for a revolution just before he was tragically assassinated and he had the support and backing of Napoleon Bonaparte of France.

These three individuals are not only heroes of the prefecture of Laconia, but are also heroes of the Greek nation. They helped their region, in which they lived and were based out of, and they also helped their own country for the cause of freedom. Also, all are connected or have some sort of ties, (whether it is family related or something else), in which it will be mentioned and described in detail within this book. Zaharias and Anagnostopoulos-Barbitsiotis were born in the same village of Varvitsa, which is located high up the Parnon Mountains of Laconia near the Laconian-Arcadian border. Back during that time period, the village of Varvitsa was known as Barbitsa (hence the name Barbitsiotis as someone who comes from Barbitsa). Nikolopoulos was born in the village of Logastra, located Northwest of Sparti, on the Taygetos Mountains of Laconia. Also, it must be mentioned that the other connection that these men had was that they taught other rebels and future klephtic leaders on diplomacy, military skills and tactics on how to fight the Turks.

This book is broken out into six different chapters. Chapter one gives a brief overview of the situation in Greece prior to the time of Zaharias, Nikolopoulos, and Anagnostopoulos-Barbitsiotis and describes what were the major historical events during that era. In addition, a brief explanation of Greek society during the time of the occupation by the Ottoman Empire and definitions to certain terms and titles (society structure) so that the readers can have a better understanding since they will be used continuously throughout the book. Chapter two, three and four will cover the life history of Zaharias, Nikolopoulos, and Anagnostopoulos-Barbitsiotis respectively (the one on Zaharias will be very brief since his life history is very long and glorious, in which that would take up one entire book alone). Chapter five mentions about the villages of Varvitsa and Logastra. Finally, Chapter six will have a conclusion as well as three poems (one for each hero) which I wrote.

Hopefully, this book will educate people not only of Greek descent, but also non-Greeks as well. It is important that we honor and pay tribute those who fought for freedom, who fought for their children and future generations, who fought for us. They deserve tremendous respect by the people and the governments. These heroes deserve more than just to have books written about them. We have the responsibility to teach ourselves and educate our children and future generations of who these heroes were and the important role they played in history and in society. This is one way of making sure that our culture and heritage passes on to the future generations.

CHAPTER ONE

In order to be able to understand and grasp the history and what went on in Greece during the time of the Ottoman occupation and before the Greek War of Independence of 1821, one must first be able to understand the social structure, and economic conditions. Also, the different problems and conditions that the Greek people had to go through during these harsh times. Therefore, this chapter will mention all of this, plus it will cover definitions to certain titles and terminology that was used in this era of Greek Modern History. The titles and terminology will be used frequently throughout the book. In addition, the second half of this chapter will cover major historical events during the Ottoman occupation of Greece leading up to the lives of Zaharias, Nikolopoulos, and Barbitsiotis up to the Greek revolution of 1821. It must be noted that the social structure and historical events that will be described pertain mainly to the southern part of Greece known as the Peloponnese. This is because the focus of the book is on the lives of these three great heroes, who not only came from this region, but also made a tremendous impact throughout the Peloponnese, and of course, Greece.

The social and government structure in the Peloponnese was somewhat different than that of Central (Roumeli) or Northern Greece. Since the Turks were more numerous in Central or Northern Greece, they were much in control of implementing and executing governmental authority, subordinate of course to the Turkish Sultan of Constantinople. On the other hand, in the Peloponnese, the Turkish community was not as large, so therefore the local Greeks and Turks held positions of authority (again being subordinate to the Turkish Sultan of Constantinople). These

Greek notables who held positions of authority in the Peloponnese were well off financially, and most were considered of an "aristocratic class." Many of the notables crossed religion boundaries, in which they actually converted to Islam for the sake of either getting a position of power, or being promoted to a higher position, or getting an increase in compensation from the Turkish government.

After the Turks defeated the Venetians in 1715, it enabled them to take control of the entire Peloponnese except for a small portion of land located in the southern tip of Laconia known as Mani. The governmental hierarchy, which the Ottoman Turks implemented for the Peloponnese was as follows: The governor or overseer, who was always Turkish, for the entire region of the Peloponnese was known as Mora Valesis or Vizer. The Mora Valesis or Vizer would report directly to the Turkish Sultan of Constantinople. Underneath the Vizer would be two Turkish Pashas who were in charge of security for the major regions of the Peloponnese. The Peloponnese was carved up into 24 different regions with its original capital being the city of Nafplio, only to be later moved to Tripoli (between 1785-1786), located in central part of the Peloponnese. The capital city was where the Vizer was always based. Every region had their own local governor known as Voevonta, their own supreme judge, and their own military commander known as Bouloubasis, who would oversee security matters in their own respected regions. Also, every town and village would elect their own representative, known as Demogerontes, who in turn would elect, on an annual basis, two Greek political representatives for their respected regions, which carried the title of Kotsabasides. In addition, all of the Kotsabasides in the entire Peloponnese (48 in all) would elect two of their colleges who would become known as Moragiannides. The Turkish Vizer, along with the two Pashas, the two Moragiannides and a Greek interpreter would form a council, in which case they would handle all major matters concerning the Peloponnese.

There was another "branch" that made up the governmental hierarchy, which was considered quite extraordinary. Two representatives from the Peloponnese, known as Veikeilides, were based in Constantinople, in which they would discuss issues concerning their home region with the Turkish Sultan. These so-called Veikeilides were sent to Constantinople in the beginning against their own free will. However, as the years passed, they became very powerful and they would play an influential role in the political affairs of the Peloponnese.

Most of the revenues raised in the Peloponnese were done by collecting taxes. At that time, the word that was used to describe money or currency was louphedes. The Turks and the Greeks who converted to Islam were not obligated to pay any taxes to the Turkish authorities. Taxes were levied on every Greek Christian male over the age of 16. Women and all handicapped individuals were also not obligated to pay any taxes. Tax payments were based on the amount of land that was farmed and / or that was used as a living space for the family. But taxes were also levied against the amount of crops that were grown and other goods that were produced by the Greeks. Most of the Greeks did not outright own the land, but worked as "serfs" on the land for their Turkish (or even sometimes Greek) masters. The tax system was completely unfair and biased as it did not favor the poor Greeks at all and made their lives even more harsh and miserable. But what made it even worse was that the local Turkish and Greek authorities, who held some form of political power, would on many occasions abuse their power and take more tax payments than was obligated from the poor Greeks so that they would keep it for themselves.

It must be mentioned here about the major role that the Greek Orthodox Church played during the Turkish occupation. One of their biggest accomplishments was that the church was able to hold together and remain united throughout the "dark ages" of the Greek people. The church did not lose touch with the people and the people did not lose touch with their faith. Its astonishing that the church was not only able to survive during these harsh times of Greece being under the Turkish yoke, but also the fact that the church was able to spread and keep the Christian faith. Another pivotal role that the church played was in education. Mainly priests would conduct classes in various secret venues, in which they became known as "secret schools", in order to teach young children about the Greek language, history, culture and religion. There were many Greek priests and religious leaders who defied the Turkish occupation and who fought in the Greek War of Independence of 1821.

The set of principles established for the social structure and for the government of the Peloponnese may seem somewhat biased against the Christian Greek Community. In reality, it was a lot worse than one can possibly imagine. The Greeks were not only discriminated by the Ottoman Turks, but there were also numerous reports of torture, false imprisonment, rape, cold blooded murders, kidnapping, and not to mention being robbed at gunpoint. The Greeks lived in fear for so many centuries. Sure, there were a few exceptions where some Greeks lived well off and didn't experience any problems (mostly Greeks who converted to Islam). And it is fair to say that not all Turks behaved in such barbaric manner. But overall it was no picnic for the "enslaved" Greek people. There was even fear of practicing their own faith, since there were many instances of religious hatred crimes against the church and its Christian congregation. The Ottoman Turks would threaten the lives of priests, religious leaders and the Greek Christian population, destroy images and icons, and even went so far as to burn churches and monasteries. Something had to give sooner or later. The Greeks decided to rebel, to push back the Turks and fight tyranny for the sake of freedom.

The Greeks were able to rebel by heading up the various mountains throughout Greece and forming guerilla-fighting units, which were called klephtes and armatoloi. Simply put, klephtes literally means robbers or thieves, which is a term in which the Turks originally called these Greek rebels. The reason for this is because these Greek rebels started off very small in that they had a tendency to steal livestock, small goods or money belonging to Turks. Greeks who supported the Turks were not immune to any "strikes" by the klephtes. As the years passed on, the actions by the klephtes increased in intensity and frequency, while at the same time, the number of Greeks joining these klephtic bands also increased. They became widespread and scattered throughout the Hellenic lands. The number of klephtes within one unit would usually average between 50 and 300. Each unit had a leader who had the title of "Kapetan" (synonymous with the title of Captain). The klephtes would not allow themselves to be subjected to Turkish tyranny. As they got stronger, they would use guerilla tactics to fight the Ottoman military power. They fought for their freedom, for the freedom of the Greek people and for the freedom of Greece. Because of their heroic deeds, they became folklore heroes, and to the eyes of the poor Greeks, who were living under Turkish tyranny, they were viewed as a sort of saviors and protectors. They were the hope for the future and for the people who were suffering daily. They were the beacons of light, the silver linen in the dark clouds. Also, since the klephtes would steal from the rich, and give to the poor, they were also viewed as the "Robin Hoods" of Greece. In essence, the klephtes became the freedom fighters of Greece.

The armatoloi were more common in Central and Northern Greece. In the Peloponnese, the armatoloi existed before 1715, when it was under control of the Venetians. After 1715, when Turks re-occupied the Peloponnese, they basically eliminated the armatoloi. The armatoloi were very similar to the klephtes, except for the fact that they would be hired and compensated by the Turks for the purpose of having them protect their properties and their own lives. In addition, the armatoloi would protect the Turkish tax collectors and certain key strategic roads and mountain passes. They became a legal security or protecting force within their respected regions. But their tasks were usually short lived (for any number of reasons), so they would switch and become klephtes. Therefore the structure of the klephtes and armatoloi were the same.

Since the klephtes and armatoloi had a tendency of switching back and forth (for a period of time they were klephtes and then would switch to armatoloi whenever it suited them and vice versa), the two words became synonymous. The klephtes and armatoloi became the armed resistance of the Greek people against the Ottoman Empire, in which it led to a battle hardened Greek force that fought for freedom before and during the Greek War of Independence. It must be mentioned that the armatoloi were nearly eliminated from the Peloponnese after 1715. The only period that armatoloi existed in the Peloponnese was during the leadership and power of Kapetan Zaharias, who formed a klephto-armatoloi federation (with him being the commander-in-chief) between 1785 and the time of his assassination in 1803-1804. The purpose of the federation was to unite all the Greek rebels for the freedom of the Peloponnese and the rest of the Hellenic world. More about this will be discussed in the next chapter.

The major historical events that will be mentioned, will actually be beneficial in providing an understanding of what went on in Greece (especially in the Peloponnese) during the days of the Ottoman occupation and the harsh living conditions being experienced – leading up to the time of Zaharias, Nikolopoulos and Barbitsiotis.

The occupation of Greece by the Ottoman Empire came about

because in May 1453, the majestic city of Constantinople (today it is known as Istanbul) fell to the conquering Ottoman Turks. Constantinople was the capital city of the Byzantine Empire, and even though it was very well fortified, the army defending the city was too small and no match for the heavily outnumbered Turks. The Emperor of the Byzantine Empire was Constantine Palaiologos who was not only the last Byzantine Emperor, but the only one not to be crowned in Constantinople (he was crowned in Mystra, located in the prefecture of Laconia), died fighting the Turks. Thus the Byzantine Empire collapsed after 11 centuries of existence. Eventually, the Ottoman Turks were able to conquer the other parts of the Byzantine Empire, such as the Balkans and Greece.

Even though the Greeks were under foreign occupation, there were still a few revolts throughout Greece during the early years under the Turkish yoke. One revolt was by Krokodeilos Kladas, who was an armatolos, in which he gathered a force of about 16 thousand men and was able to defeat the Turks in many battles in the harsh region of Mani, located in Laconia. The 16 thousand men were made up by a united rebel force of Kladas and a fellow armatolos by the name of Theodoros Bouas from Nafplio. Unfortunately, because of constant disagreements, Kladas and Bouas decided to part ways, in which case it was not long before their revolt against the Turks came to an end.

A major event, which occurred during the 16th century, was the naval battle of Nafpaktos. On October 7 1571, a combined naval force from Venetia and Spain annihilated the entire Turkish navy, which took part in this battle. This caused many Greeks throughout the land to rise up and revolt. In the Peloponnese, a revolt was spearheaded by the Melissini family along with the religious leader, Archbishop Makarios. The revolt, which lasted for about two years, was concentrated basically in the Mani region. They were hoping for military assistance by a European nation(s), but when it was evident that foreign help would not arrive, they decided to terminate their revolt. The Turks ran amok, and they tortured, butchered (over 30,000 Greeks were killed), burned villages, and imprisoned people in retaliation of the ensuing revolts.

There were also planned revolts and revolutions, which unfortunately never developed. For example, on October 8 1612, the most powerful and influential families in Mani wrote and signed a letter, which was sent to France, asking for military assistance in order to start a revolution against the Ottoman Turks and free Greece. The families that signed the letter were Kontostavlon, Niklon, and Kosmas. However, because of bickering with other nations in Europe, France was never able to provide a meaningful and substantial military assistance to Mani.

From 1684-1715, there were ongoing wars between the Venetians (and her allies) against the Ottoman Empire. The Venetians had called upon the Greeks for help in fighting the Turks, and the first to respond to action in the Peloponnese were the Maniates (from Mani of course). The first group of wars lasted until 1698 when the defeated Turks sued for peace and the victorious Venetians attained the Peloponnese. But the peace did not last long, as another war flared up between the two rivals in 1715, only this time the Turks were victorious and got back the Peloponnese from the Venetians.

The next major event during the 18th century was the so-called "Orlov Rebellion" of 1770. The rebellion came about because in 1768 Russia declared war on the Ottoman Empire and they were hoping to help the Greeks start some sort uprising so that the Turks would have to fight a multi-front war. In February 1770, a small Russian contingent arrived in Greece, headed by Theodoro Orlov (specifically they arrived in the Mani region) to oversee the rebellion which was started by the Maniates. But

16

the whole rebellion was very unorganized, ill prepared, and a complete fiasco. Despite the initial success that the small rebellion force achieved, they could not withstand the Turkish counterattacks, or the Albanians, which were recruited from outside the Peloponnese in order to assist the Turks in this conflict. The rebellion was crushed, the Russians left, and the Turks (along with the Albanians) went on a rampage seeking revenge, and ended up slaughtering over 3,000 Greeks. From the beginning, there were major problems with the "Orlov Rebellion." In addition to the problems mentioned above, the very small Greek force combined with an even smaller Russian force sealed the fate of this uprising. The other problem was that the Russians had promised the Greeks that they would send a very large force, with an abundance of military supplies. But none of this ever came about.

The Greeks in the Peloponnese lived in terrible conditions and in constant fear after the disaster with the "Orlov Rebellion." Between 1770-1779, the newly settled Albanians devastated the entire region of the Peloponnese. They murdered, raped, and abducted innocent victims, while at the same time, burned towns and villages. The most common crime they committed was armed robbery. As if this wasn't enough, the Albanians started to commit these same crimes against their so-called allies, the Turks. Because of this, in 1779, the Sultan of Constantinople sent the Turkish naval commander Hasan Tzetzarli to the Peloponnese to chase out the Albanians and bring order to the region. The Turks decided to form an alliance with the Greek klephtes of the Peloponnese, since it was also in their best interest to get rid of the Albanians. The war was a complete success for the Turks and the Greek klephtes. They defeated and chased out most of the Albanians form the region (not all of the Albanians left the Peloponnese). The Turks and the Greek klephtes killed over five thousand Albanians, in which all of their heads were cut off and were used to build a "pyramid of skulls" outside of the city of Tripoli. The klephtes, which were led by Constantine

Kolokotronis (father of Theodoros Kolokotronis, hero of the Greek War of Independence of 1821) suffered about 100-150 casualties. The Turkish – Greek alliance achieved a great victory. But this alliance was short lived.

In 1780, the Turks went against the Greek klephtes. The Turks requested the klephtes to submit to the government authorities, in return they would get some sort of amnesty. Most of the klephtes did submit, except for Kolokotronis, Panagiotaros and a few others. Both of these men and their rebel forces, along with their families, remained united together and situated in the village of Kastania, (the home village of Panagiotaros) located in the Mani region of Laconia. A Turkish force of about six thousand went to Kastania and attacked the forts of Panagiotaros, which was defended by about 150 klephtes. The siege lasted for about 12 days, when the klephtes decided to come out of the forts, charge at the Turks, and hopefully not have all of the Greeks perish in this bloody conflict. Few managed to escape, including Theodoros Kolokotronis, who was about 10 years old, and his mother. The klephtic leaders, Panagiotaros Venetsenakis and Constantine Kolokotronis, were killed by the Turks after they made their exodus from the forts.

CHAPTER TWO

This Chapter will focus on the history of Kapetan Zaharias and the significant role he played for Greece during his lifetime. The scope here is just to outline and highlight some of the major points and events, and not go into the subject matter deeper or give an extended analysis. The history of Zaharias is very long and glorious; in which a huge book by itself would be needed in order to explain the history in more detail.

Zaharias was born on October 22, 1759 in the village of Varvitsa in Laconia, Greece. His family name (surname) was Pantelakos - Pagonis and his father's name was Theodoros. Later on in his life he would be known as Zaharias Barbitsiotis (Varvitsiotis), since he originally came from the village of Barbitsa (Varvitsa). It was not uncommon for individuals living during this era to take on the name of the village or region they came from and include it as part of their name. Someone, for example, might have been addressed as "Maniates" because they came from the region of Mani, or "Tripolitsotis" because they came from the town of Tripoli.

As a young lad, he got a job working as a sheepherder for a wealthy Turkish landowner in the village of Agio Petros, which is located in the Kynoria region of Arcadia. But Zaharias father took him out of this job and gave him the responsibility of being a sheepherder on a piece of land they owned in Arcadia. Even at this young age Zaharias was showing signs of greatness. He went to the butcher shop one time to get some meat for his family whereby he asked the butcher for the price of the meat. After the butcher told him the amount, Zaharias then said if he could have the meat for nothing by cutting it with his own little dagger. The butcher, believing that this little boy with his little dagger would probably be able to cut a piece of meat the size of a small finger, agreed. Zaharias with his incredible strength was able to cut a large chunk of meat, which he threw over his shoulder and went home.

Zaharias father, Theodoros, was killed by the Turks (via betrayal by a co-villager) around 1774. Theodoros was the godfather of Theodoros Kolokotronis in that, it is believed, is how the young Kolokotronis got his first name. The family of Zacharias had close ties with the Kolokotronis family, which is probably the reason why Zaharias father, Theodoros, baptized Theodoros Kolokotronis. The two-klephtic families struggled constantly against the Turkish oppressors and wanted no sooner than to see Greece gain her freedom. Zaharias father was a klepht and became a member of Kapetan Panagiotaras unit, which was based in Mani (some believe that he was second in command of the unit of Panagiotaras). Theodoros took part in the unsuccessful uprising of 1770 called the "Orlov Revolution." He had close contact with Bishop Ananias Lambardis from Dimitsana (Arcadia) who was one of the organizers of this revolution. Theodoros acted as a correspondent or a "middleman" in which he informed Kapetan Constantine Kolokotronis, and the Maniates of the planned uprising. When the "Orlov Revolution" failed, the Turks went amok throughout the Peloponnese. They would track down the Greek klephtes and do battle against them or they would capture well-known klephtes in their respective villages in which they would execute them. This action by the Turks lasted for a few years. Theodoros was not able to escape the Turkish wrath. He was captured and executed for taking part in the "Orlov Revolution."

Zaharias older brother, Pantelis was also killed by the Turks in

1774 or 1775 in the village of Varvitsa. It is believed that Pantelis was about 17 or 18 years of age at the time he was killed. This tragedy occurred after the "Orlov Revolution" and at a time when the Turks were going after Greek rebels and other Greeks who may have been involved in this unsuccessful revolution in some way or another. The killing of his older brother had a profound affect on Zaharias, which changed his life forever. He was naturally angry by what happened to his family members, and at the same time revengeful. He wanted to dedicate his entire life killing Turks and seeing Greece gain her independence.

In 1776, Zaharias joined the rebel unit headed by Kapetan Matzari from Logastra, Laconia (who was, however, originally from Tegea, Arcadia). According to historians, Zaharias approached Matzari with the intention of joining his rebel group, in which he said to him that his family members were killed by the Turks and that he wants to devote his entire life killing Turks. Matzari said to Zaharias that he was "young, too young, very very young." Zaharias replied that he has a big heart and soul, which will be revealed during battle. Some historians indicate a slightly different account in which Kapetan Matzari asked Zaharias what is his name, where is he from, and what does he want. "Zaharias from Varvitsa," he replied and also stated that he wanted to kill Turks. Matzari asked him if he ever killed before, to which Zaharias said that he does not have any weapons. Matzari then gave him two or three weapons to Zaharias, which he took, but immediately fled with lightning speed. The next morning he went back to Matzari and brought to him two decapitated Turkish heads. Matzari did not hesitate to accept Zaharias into the rebel unit. His stay in Matzari's unit would not last long.

In 1777, Zaharias went to Matzari in which he told him that the Turks from Leontari, located in the region of Arcadia, are coming after him and that the they were positioned in the monastery Rokitsa. Matzari ordered his men, who were situated, near the region of Leontari, to get ready to march to Rokitsa to fight the Turks. The men marched during the night and were able to reach the monastery by dawn. The monastery Rokitsa is located about seven kilometers from the village of Dirrahi located in the Southern Arcadia region. Today, only the small church of St.George remains intact. During the battle, Zaharias took his sword out and with his powerful voice ordered to charge (against the wishes of Kapetan Matzari) resulting in the Turks being put to flight and the Greeks winning the battle. According to the sources, 9 Greek rebels and 27 Turks were killed.

Kapetan Matzari was angry after the battle because of the fact that Zaharias did not follow his orders. In addition, Matzari's anger grew even more when, it was decided by his men, that Zaharias should get most of the loot for his bravery during the battle, and for leading the decisive attack against the Turks. Zaharias and the men of Kapetan Matzari also decided to give a portion of the loot to the monastery Rokitsa. The loot (military arms, supplies, food, etc) was mainly what the Turks had left behind from the battlefield.

The rebel unit split when Zaharias (along with 60 other rebels) left Kapetan Matzari to form his own unit in which he was recognized as Kapetan. He organized his unit very well, he appointed a sergeant of arms, a secretary, and formed his own flag. The flag was tricolor in that the top bar had a red color, the middle bar was white, and the bottom bar was black. In the middle of the flag (the white bar) he had a blue cross with the words Liberty or Death written in blood above the cross. He would later add his own personal label, which was located in the bottom of the flag with the words "Commander in Chief of the Peloponnese." It is believed that the red color in Zaharias flag symbolized blood, while the white color stood for freedom and the black stood for death. Zaharias was the second Greek to form his own flag for the independence of Greece from the Turkish yoke. But his flag may have been the first to have the sign of the cross, the symbol of Christianity. It must be pointed out that amazingly Zaharias did all of this at a time when he was barely 18 years of age.

In 1781, Zaharias led a march to Leondari with his unit when they passed through the village of Upper Salesi in Arcadia. This actual site is located today near the village of Makrisi, just east of the city of Megalopoli. According to the historical sources, after Zaharias positioned his unit in Upper Salesi, the Turks saw the unit with an open flag (in which they had never seen before) and sent a messenger to the village of Leondari. The Turks of Leondari came upon the village of Salesi and positioned themselves in Lower Salesi. They then sent one of their police guards to Upper Salesi to find out about the unit, who are they, and what are they doing here. After finding out, the Turkish police guard returned back to his commander and said that they told him they were men of Zaharias. The Turks then sent the police guard back to tell Zaharias to take down his flag and for him and his unit to come down and bow (be subdued) to Isouf- aga Zante the local governor. If he should not comply, then the local Turks will send for the Turkish commander and chief of the military forces for the region who is known by the name of Tziko to bring their heads. Zaharias then sends a letter and says the following: "(To) Isouf-aga Zante, local governor. You ordered us to come down and be subdued by you. We are not brides! Get up, and get out of here before you become a donkey, because my name is Zaharias (from) Varvitsiotis. You mentioned to take down our flag... We will take down your heads, because (our flag) has a cross with the words (written) in blood: liberty or death. I tell you this since you are governor, send me 300 louphedes (currency money/coins) for my men. If you do not send me this, I will use my sword on your heads and burn your properties." The 300 louphedes currency means that Zaharias had 300 men with him at that time since the louphedes would be divided up by each man getting one apiece. Isouf-aga Zante got angry when he read Zaharias letter. The Turkish commander Tziko arrived with his troops. The battle began and lasted for almost the entire afternoon. Tziko then decided to charge at Zaharias and Zaharias decided to charge at Tziko. As the two men approached each other Zaharias was able to cut down Tziko with his sword. Zaharias then yells out to his men; "Charge at them men, we will take the Turks!" The Turks were routed and had to withdraw from the battlefield. According to the sources 70 Turks were killed, while for the Greeks 22 lost their lives. The men of Zaharias were able to collect plenty of goods the Turks had left behind from the battlefield. After the battle Zaharias and his unit marched on to the village of Xerovouna, located on the Taygetos Mountains on the border of Messinia and Laconia.

After the great victory for Zaharias in Salesi, the Nikolopoulos family from Logastra came to congratulate Zaharias and they made an oath to him, in which they pledged their full support and that they will bring anything he needs from Mistra. Zaharias told them that he needs led (bullets), gunpowder, rocks, and leather shoes. In addition, he told them that money and bread he could get with his sword. He also asked the municipality of Leondari for 3,000 louphedes and to recognize his unit as a unit of armatoloi. He further organized his unit by appointing his cousin Anastasios Koulomertzilos from Varvitsa, who would become a trusted advisor, and Demetrios Kallotzin from Sitainis as first officers. Also, he appointed Yannis Bouloukos from Varvitsa as flag bearer.

Zaharias stayed in the village of Xerovouna for about a year. In 1782, he married a relative of the Nikolopoulos family (probably an arranged marriage) in which her first name was Pagona and she was from the village of Logastra (her family roots were from Pigadia, located in the western Mani region). After this he decided to leave Xerovouna so that he may continue with a more effective campaign against the Turks in order to gain liberty for Greece and its people.

Zaharias went back with his unit to his home village of Varvitsa. He used some of the louphedes to pay his men while the remaining balance he used to build two forts in the village of Varvitsa. The two forts had a rectangle shape and were three stories long. The forts were in close proximity of each other, in which there was an overhead bridge that connected one with the other. In addition, their average size was about 12 meters long and were both completed in the year 1783. The impact of this was an increase of power for Zaharias over the entire region, while at the same time, he was hoping that the local politicians would recognize him as armatoloi leader. Such recognition would qualify him to receive compensation (which he would pay his men) from the local politicians to oversee the security over the region. Should he receive more money and wealth, it would cause an increase in his power, strength, and influence. But the Turkish officials in the Laconian region were very much alarmed by the actions of Zaharias. So much so that the Turks decided to go on an offensive campaign and attack Zaharias and his forts in Varvitsa.

The Turks and their supporters made three separate attacks on Varvitsa, hoping to get rid of Zaharias, in which they all occurred in the year 1783. All of the attacks Zaharias was able to repel and beat the Turks. A ballard was written and sung after Zaharias incredible charge and attack on the Turks whose commander, named Kouleles from the village of Prastou (located in the region of Kynoria in Arcadia), was beaten by Zaharias. Kouleles was a powerful figure in the region during that time and it is believed that he was of Greek origin but converted to Islam. The following verses pertain to this particular ballad:

The snow shines on the mountains, like the sun does the sky.
Just like Zaharias shines from all the other warriors.
The Tsakonitika Mountains are very foggy.
The northern wind blows, the winters are harsh.
No one set foot from the old klephtes.
Zaharias walks and sets foot on them.
Zaharias enjoys it with Koulomertzilos.
In front walks Zaharias, behind him is Koulomertzilos.
In the middle is Kalliotzis, like the warrior he is.
They go (walk on) rock to rock.
They went and set across the field.
They sit and write a letter to Kouleles:
"To you Kouleles and Demetraki,
Why don't you send me the louphedes which you owe me?"
Kouleles writes back: "We send you bread and shoes,
We do not owe you any louphedes,
Led bullets, gun powder we have and we will share it (among ourselves)."
Zaharias read the letter and smiles:
"We will now go to Prastou to the forts of Kouleles,
Take the louphedes as much as you can,
I will take the women so that I may kiss them."
The battle began, the muskets started firing.
They injured Kalliontzis (in the battle).

After the battles of 1783, Zaharias was starting to become famous all across the land. His power and influence was increasing, while at the same time, he was enforcing a calm and hope to the villages throughout the region of Laconia. The klephtes and other Greeks were singing songs in his name, and dancing in his honor all across the regions. One popular song, which was sung during this time period had the following lyrics:

I give my oath to my sword,
The cross is my charm.
Turk that I may find and kill,
So that I may free a Greek.

Since Kapetan Zaharias was achieving great success against the Turkish tyrants, men were coming from all parts just to join his unit and fight under his flag, which was the flag for the freedom of Greece. In 1785, Zaharias came up with a great idea, which would become one of his greatest projects and achievements in his lifetime. Zaharias idea was to form a klephto-armatoloi federation, which would encompass the entire region of the Peloponnese. The problem with Greece and the Greeks at this time (and previous generations) was that it was very difficult for the Greek rebels (klephtes/armatoloi) to unite as one army and fight a united front against the Turks. The reason was either because the rebel groups in their respected regions were fighting for their own interests, or there was no one great leader who would step up and form a united front to try to lead the Greeks to their freedom. This was the aim of Zaharias, he wanted to fight the Turks on a united front so he can free the Peloponnese, and once this had been accomplished, he would then turn his attention to free the rest of Greece. He started by enlisting the Kapetans (Captains) and their units, from the entire region of the Peloponnese into the federation, while at the same time Zaharias would be recognized as commander and leader of the Peloponnese and the federation. He would then keep in close contact and communicate with the Kapetans (Captains) of all the regions of the Peloponnese, as they would also keep in close contact with him, in which they would share information of any enemy advancement or any decisions or by the local Turkish leaders. Zaharias would also communicate to the Kapetans from the other regions as to what tactics they should deploy, what actions should they take, and how should they do it. In addition, Zaharias would not only teach the other Kapetans about tactics and military strategy, but he would also teach them about diplomacy. The principal and most effective tactic which Zaharias used for the federation was when one region was coming under attack from the Turks, then all of the other regions would be notified of this and they, in turn, would start attacking Turkish positions in their respected regions. The impact of this was that the Turks from the other regions would not be able to send any troops or reinforcements to help out their comrades in the original region which the battle(s) took place. The formation of the federation would mark a turning point in Modern Greek history. The reason was that the Greek rebels were being united and were fighting for a common cause with a united front. In addition, the Greek rebels had now a great leader and a great military commander to look up to with the hope that freedom and liberty would be achieved after centuries of Turkish occupation.

In the autumn of the same year of 1785, Theodoros Kolokotronis decided to pay a visit to Kapetan Zaharias at his home village of Varvitsa. At the time of this visit, Kolokotronis was only 15 years of age. When Kolokotronis arrived, Zaharias recognized him from the very beginning. "You must be Kolokotronis," Zaharias said. "How did you know?" responded Kolokotronis. Zaharias replied "I recognize your face." Zaharias knew the father of Theodoros Kolokotronis, Constantine, and since Theodoros had a close resemblance to his father, it was obvious that Zaharias would recognize him from the beginning. Both men sat and talked, Zaharias gave a feast with lamb roasting on a spit. Kolokotronis mentions in his memoirs that he was very much impressed with Zaharias. According to Kolokotronis, when he arrived at Varvitsa, he never had seen a leader or a man like Zaharias before. Zaharias was a great leader, very well organized, and a great tactician. Kolokotronis was impressed with the physical attributes and condition of Zaharias (more on this subject will be mentioned later). In addition, Kolokotronis admired the way Zaharias men were very well trained, well organized, and disciplined. Kolokotronis also mentioned that Zaharias would assume the role of a judge, in which, he would settle disputes and decide on criminal cases by following the law books of the old Byzantine Empire called "Armenopoulo." These law books were called "Armenopoulo" because they were written by Constantine Armenopoulos, who lived in the 14th century in Greece during the Byzantine era. Armenopoulos, whose writings was mostly published during the 16th century, wrote extensively about laws and set guidelines on how to judge cases. These laws and guidelines were carried out and abided in many parts of Greece for centuries.

During the formation of the federation Zaharias, as general commander, appointed Theodoros Kolokotronis and Athanasios Petimazas as second in command. Athanasios Petimazas was from the Kalavrita region of the Peloponnese and he to was a young and competent Kapetans in which he earned the respect from his men in their respected region. Some of the other Kapetan who agreed to join Zaharias klephto-armatoloi federation were: Matzari (the same Matzari mentioned in chapter one), Nikolopoulos from Logastra, Athanasios Karabela from Vervenian, Makroyiannis from Thelposis, Koulospyrou from Arkoudorema, and Anagnostaras from Arcadia. The ambassador for the federation was Yiannias from the Photakon region of Achaia.

The three main bylaws of the federation were as follows: First, for the federation to be recognized by all of the 24 regions of the Peloponnese as a single Greek armatoloi unit, so that it may oversee the security of the Peloponnese, while at the same time, receive economic support from the Turkish lords/political leaders who preside in those regions. Second, must be sure that the economic support they receive must not come from tax revenues the Turkish lords/political leaders collect from their respected regions so as to not burden the poor Greek civilians. Third, elec-

29

tions to be held in all the regions of the Peloponnese for the position of region Kapetan in accordance with the laws of the federation. Of course, the primary principle of the federation was to plan for the freedom of the Peloponnese. Varvitsa became the home base of the federation when it was first formed. In effect, Varvitsa became the center for Greek klephtes, during the first couple of years of the federation, whose goal and ambition was to start a revolution to free Greece.

Some historians believe that after the formation of the federation, Zaharias began to proclaim himself as General or Commander in Chief of the Peloponnese. In his official correspondences and letters to the other Kapetans, members of the federation, and to Turkish officials, he would sign his name and write Commander in Chief of the Peloponnese. He added his own personalized label in the bottom of the flag, which stated his name and included the words "Commander in Chief of the Peloponnese." With this title, Zaharias became the first Greek Commander in Chief since the fall of the Byzantine Empire in 1453.

By the spring of 1786, the federation had been very well organized and was receiving cooperation from the klephtes/armatoloi of the entire Peloponnese region. Zaharias sent a letter to the Kotsabasides for the main purpose of the federation being recognized as a security force by them. In the letter Zaharias says: "You should pay the louphedes to my men, so that you won't see any uprisings all the time. Do not collect or overburden the poor with taxes in order to pay my men and me. They are innocent and they have not harmed me. Pay me, or I will set fire, (and use my) sword against the Turks. Understand well, I will continue to do this. I will also tell you this, that the Turkish judges should judge and decide (cases) only for the Turks, and not the Greeks. The Greeks will be judged by me, and the Turks by the Turkish judges. You write to me that your villages will be destroyed...

30

ashes they should become! Muskets and swords! Either liberty or death!"

The Kotsabasides replied with the following letter: "Kapetan Zaharias! Don't destroy the villages. The (Greek) warriors have not long to live and that is because the Turkish leaders (in the Peloponnese) are very angry with you. They hear your steps and you better start worrying." Zaharias responded with another letter: "The blood of my brother yells out. The Turks (in the battle of) Rokitsa are moaning...(battles of) Salesi, Varvitsa (he is mentioning his past battles). You (Kotsabasides) should support me so that I may become a protector of the Christians. I have many comrades that should be paid so that we won't start an uprising.

As the one month deadline was approaching for Zaharias to receive the louphedes, villagers from Kastri, located in the region of Kynoria in Arcadia, went to Zaharias to express their fears of what was happening in their village. They said that a mourtati (a Greek converted to Islam) by the name of Loumanis is plundering their village, and he is kidnapping young children and women in order to convert them to Islam by force. Zaharias then ordered his sergeant in arms to take ten men and to go to the village of Kastri, so that they may bring Loumanis head to him. The men captured Loumanis, tied him up, and brought him to the top of the mountain. When news of this leaked out, there was a sense of euphoria among the villagers of the region. However, when the Kotsabasides heard what happened, they sent a letter to Zaharias asking him to release Loumanis because they were afraid that the Turks would cause chaos among the Greek leaders reporting under their Turkish bosses. Zaharias response was: "You can have his body which is located on the mountain. But I need to talk to his head, for I heard he has big brains and much influence in Turkey." Indeed, the men had cut Loumanis head off and brought it to their Kapetan.

The Kotsabasides who sent the letter to Zaharias asking for the release of Loumanis, was none other than Protopapa and Kondakis of Agio Petro. Protopapa, who was a priest, would eventually become a much-hated enemy of Zaharias, while Kondakis, on the other hand, had great respect for him and would later on become good friends. In addition, Kondakis wrote extensively about Zaharias in his memoirs. After the execution of Loumanis, Zaharias decided to send a letter to the Kotsabasides who asked for the release of Loumanis. In the letter Zaharias writes: "Send me three pairs of leather shoes, ammunition (gun powder, led, etc.) and 2,000 louphedes. Should you dare not send them, I will then come to your village and I will double it." This letter was sort of a "punishment" for the Kotsabasides for their supportive role of Loumanis. Kondakis gave his share of what Zaharias asked for in his letter. But Protopapa would not pay up. Kondakis mentioned to Zaharias that Protopapa would not pay his share, in which case Zaharias decided to punish Protopapa. Zaharias captured Protopapa's two sons who were very supportive of Loumanis and would help carry out his ruthless deeds. Zaharias killed one of the sons, and the other he held for ransom, which he received.

The Greek ballad below pertains to what happened between Zaharias and Protopapa. This version was published in French by C. C. Fauriel and later translated into English by Charles Brinsley Sheridan of England, during the time the Greek War of Independence was in full swing. The lyrics show Zaharias talking and complaining about the situation with Protopapa. Here then, is the translation into English by Sheridan, which comes under the title of "The Defence of Zacharias":

> *Though all the neighboring villages*
> *With threats and clamor ring,*
> *To what amounts my fancied crime,*
> *The charge your Primates bring?*

That Proestos complains the most,
St. Peter's * lordly priest!
One might suppose that I had robb'd
The miser's herds at least:

I only kiss'd his daughter's lips –
The kiss was fairly won;
And 'twas in arm'd and manly fight
I slew his elder son;

And though I made his bags disgorge
Five hundred bits of gold,
He thus regain'd his younger boy,
Whom else I might have sold.

I gave among my gallant band
The sordid traitor's pelf;
The memory of a single kiss
Was all I kept myself."

*St. Peter is the literal English translation of the village named Agio Petro. Sheridan also translated Fauriel's comments about Zaharias, in which it is stated that "his (Zaharias) generosity and humanity towards his poorer countrymen, as fully equalling his strength, his swiftness, his fortitude, and his sagacity." In addition, Fauriel also mentioned that Zaharias came from one of the oldest families in the Peloponnese.

In April 1786, Zaharias and his men went to the monastery in Malevi, located just east of Agio Petro (in the region of Kynoria in Arcadia). Some historians believe that the reason why Zaharias went to Malevi was so as to go against and punish Protopapa (who was not far away) for his role against Zaharias. The Turks found out about Zaharias position and immediately went out after him. When Zaharias saw the Turks approaching, he decided

33

to leave the monastery so that not only would it not be damaged from the battle, but that the monks would not suffer any casualties. Zaharias took a position, not far from the monastery, which was named Darmiri. The Turks then, followed where Zaharias was positioned and a full-scale battle ensued. Zaharias was heavily outnumbered and outgunned, in which case he would run a great risk if he decided to counterattack or charge. His decision then was to hold his position and keep fighting. The battle was entering a third day, when reinforcements arrived for Zaharias. The reinforcement unit was headed by Kapetan Thanasi Karabelas. With the reinforcements intact, Zaharias decided to counterattack, and charge against the Turks. Some of the Turks threw away their arms, while the (Greek) klephtes captured 14 mules belonging to the enemy. The Turkish commander spoke from the monastery (the Turks retreated back to the monastery) in which he says, "Zaharias, cease the battle, cease firing, let us talk so that we can come to an agreement." Zaharias then orders his men to capture the monastery. The men set a "smoking screen" to the doors and stairs of the monastery so that they would be able to enter without being detected. The men were able to enter into the monastery in which they killed many Turks. The Turkish commander spoke to the monks in the hope that they can persuade Zaharias to cease the battle. The monks then spoke to Zaharias, "Zaharias cease the battle, cease firing, so that we may hold a dialogue and come to a resolution." Zaharias responds, "I do not like it, I will finish them (the Turks) all, and then I will have a dialogue and an agreement. Let them see the weapons, let them see my musket." The battle then continued and the Greeks captured many weapons, some of which were highly valued. Zaharias then decided to cease fire (to see what the Turks had to say) in which he ordered Kapetan Thanasi to cease-fire. Kapetan Thanasi was slightly injured in his hand during the battle.

When the cease-fire took into effect, the Turkish commander

said to Zaharias that he should return back to the region he came from, and not to disrupt or cause havoc in the region that they were presently in (Agio Petro). Zaharias response to the Turkish commander was as follows: "All of the regions belong to me and my country. You're country is in Mecca, go back to Mecca where you belong. I will spill my blood for my enslaved country." The historian Takis Kandeloros mentions that this is the first time a Greek commander living under Turkish occupation, confronts his enemy and tells his enemy that his objective is to spill his blood for his enslaved country and that the natural place for the Turks is in Mecca.

In the end the Turks were humiliated and Zaharias achieved another victory. Zaharias and his entire unit marched back to Varvitsa victorious just in time to celebrate the Greek Easter, in which at that year fell on the 12th of April.

A few months after the battle at Malevi, a Turkish unit from Mistra found out where Zaharias and his unit were situated, in which the Turks decided to march on to the area to do battle against Zaharias. Specifically, they marched to an area called Marinou rema (the stream of Marinou) near Vassara, in which they hoped to ambush and trap Zaharias and his unit. But this was a very difficult task for the Turks, because Zaharias was a brilliant commander and an excellent military strategist.

The Turks positioned themselves near the stream of Marinou where they hoped to ambush Zaharias and his unit as they would be crossing the stream. But when Zaharias approached the stream he divided his unit in two and he told his men to take up positions to the extreme left and right of the stream. He told his men to do this in case the Turks were positioned near the stream and were planning an ambush. With this tactic, Zaharias was outflanking the Turks on both sides, and putting them in a disadvantage position by leaving them in the middle of the ensuing battle. Zaharias was correct about the planned ambush and the position of the Turks. The battle erupted between the two sides and lasted for many hours. The Turks suffered a major defeat from this battle. The area of the battle site near the stream was later named "sphereodromion" ("bullet road") of Zaharias, which is still called even today.

In the fall of 1786, Zaharias entered the Mani region as he was going along the Evrotas River, in which he decided to settle in the village called Skoufomiti. Specifically, the village of Skoufomiti was located in the mountains of the northern region of Mani, just north from the village of Mirsini, not too far from Bardounochoron, Agios Nikolaos, and Poliaravo. Today, Skoufomiti falls under the district of Lygerea in conjunction with the village of Ano Asteri (formally known as Pano Sola) and as part of the municipality of Gytheio. It is estimated that the village was about 700 meters (nearly 2,300 feet) above sea level. This made Skoufomiti, along with the neighboring village of Poliaravo, the most elevated places in the Mani region. From Skoufomiti, one can see far out in the distance all the way to Sparta (to the north), and to Inner Mani (to the south). Today the village exists only by name, since no one lives there anymore.

In Skoufomiti, Zaharias bought land that was owned by the Vavoulianon family. Zaharias (with his family) along with his unit and their respective families settled in the village of Skoufomiti, where it too was also turned into a new base from which Zaharias could operate from against the Turks. In the village of Skoufomiti, Zaharias built two forts, a church, school, and a hospital. In addition, an irrigation system was put in place to be used for farmlands. The two forts were actually located outside the village (across from the main peak of Skoufomiti) some two and a half kilometers away. Thus, Zaharias had two peaks within his control, which enabled him to have a panoramic view of the entire region. This area is known as the "Halsmata tou Zaharia."

There was also a secret tunnel located underground from the "Halsmata tou Zaharia" which led up to the two forts. The area where the tunnel is located is known as "Trypa tou Zaharia" or Cave of Zaharia. This tunnel was used to store supplies and also as an escape route whenever it was needed. It also was used as a pathway for the klephtes to gain access to the forts in order to attack the approaching enemy. The cave itself has three exits, which were at a great distance from the forts.

The church mentioned above, which was built by Zaharias, is named Panagitsa. The dimensions are 7.50 m X 3.60 m, and was used as a place of worship for his men and their families. On one of the walls located in the back of the altar, there is a writing dated in the year 1844, which includes a list of names, one being that of Pagona. The name Pagona happens to be the name of Kapetan Zaharias wife. Pagona was his first wife, but she later died and he remarried again as will be mentioned below. It is possible that this writing in the back of the church was some sort of dedication and honor for her and for the other individuals on the list.

By relocating his base to the Mani region, Zaharias would be able to carry out his campaign against the Turks much more effectively. The combination of Mani being a very hostile region (hostile towards the Turks) plus the remote location of the region made it very difficult for the Turks to go after Zaharias. Therefore, this new position offered greater security because the Mani region spreads all along the south and east of Skoufomiti, while at the same time, the Taygetos and Parnon mountains rise up to the north.

The Turkish officials of the Peloponnese, fearing what might happen and seeing Zaharias as a major threat to them, had to come to some sort of resolution so that they would be able to handle this crisis for the time being. Their fear was that Zaharias, being more powerful, would be able to campaign and do whatever else he wants against them whenever he felt, while at the same time, it would be difficult for the Turks to go after him because of his location. Therefore, the Turkish officials and their leader, the Vizer, decided (beginning of 1787) to send a letter to Zaharias, in which they "appointed" him to the respected title of Dervenagas of the Peloponnese. This title meant that Zaharias would be a protector of the land, and would oversee security matters for the entire region of the Peloponnese. Also, the letter stated that the Turkish officials from the 24 regions (provinces) of the Peloponnese would pay Zaharias 2,000 louphedes a month as compensation and that if he does a good and satisfying job, the officials will grant him many favors. Zaharias received and read the letter, in which case he decided to send a letter of his own to three members of the federation (Petimazas, Kolokotronis, and Anagnostaras). In it he writes that the Turkish officials appointed him Dervenagas of the Peloponnese and that they should inform the other members of the federation by writing to them as well. Also, Zaharias stated that every month all of the members of the federation should send a representative in order to receive a share of the 2,000 louphedes, and that should the Turks decide to terminate their monthly payments to him, he would notify the members of the federation to start an uprising.

With this decision by the Turkish officials, it also meant that they recognized the klephto-armatoloi federation, which was one of dreams and goals of Zaharias. They realized how powerful the federation had become, and how serious the threat was to Turkish security. But the Turks hoped that this recognition would be short lived, in that by taking this action they hoped to accomplish the following: First, by recognizing the federation, and giving Zaharias the title of Dervenagas, the Turks were hoping to pacify Zaharias for a while. Second, by pacifying Zaharias, the panic and fear already in existence would subside among the Turks in the Peloponnese. Finally, with peace and tranquillity in place the Turks would have the time to focus on a plan which would hopefully eliminate Zaharias and the federation and get them out of danger.

In the letter mentioned above, which stated that Zaharias would be "appointed" to the title of Dervenagas, the Turks said that they need assistance in trying to capture a rebel leader by the name of Merakos and his followers. Merakos was a Turkish - Albanian who came from the Bardounochoron region just north of Mani. He became leader of a rebel unit, which not only included Turks but Greeks as well, and would constantly go up against the Turkish authorities in the region. Merakos was more of a highway robber in which he and his rebels would enter towns and villages in order to rob people of their money and their tangible possessions such as cattle or horses. These rebels would not discriminate as they robbed Turks and Greeks alike for their own personal interests. On many occasions their bad deeds went too far when Merakos and his rebels, upon entering a village, would physically abuse the villagers and even rape the women. It should be mentioned that another rebel Turk, who went by the name of Avdi and was from the village of Potamia (west of Dafni), had united his small force with the rebels of Merakos in which they would carry out their ruthless deeds as a combined unit.

Merakos had built a strong a fort in the village of Dafni (which was his central base) located north of Krokees in Laconia. The Turkish Pasha had already sent a small force to Dafni to try to penetrate the fort (which was situated in the center of the village) and either capture or kill Merakos and his men. The leader of this small force was a Turk by the name of Mousaga, who also was from the Bardounochoron region, in which he had been constantly attacking Merakos (who was well protected by his forts) for three months without any success.

The prolonged and unsuccessful attacks by Mousaga on Merakos prompted the Turkish Pasha to ask Zaharias, who now had the title of Dervenagas, for assistance to defeat Merakos. Without hesitation, Zaharias decided to assist Mousaga in his campaign by gathering his klephtic unit and marching to the village of Dafni to join the fight. Zacharias had great reasons as to why he should participate in this dangerous and risky operation. Merakos and his rebels were murderers, rapists, and thieves in which they were causing havoc, grief and chaos throughout the region. With this in mind, Zaharias wanted to participate in the operation and defeat Merakos in order to end the fears and suffering of the people. In addition, not only did he want to bring Merakos to justice for all the crimes he committed, but also to punish the Greek rebels who were actively involved in those crimes with Merakos. Zaharias felt that it was his duty to bring to justice the Greek rebels, because he believed that he should be the "judge" involved in deciding cases against Greeks, his own people, and not the Turks.

In his heart, the Turkish Pasha really wanted to get rid of Zaharias, his biggest and most dangerous enemy to him and to the Ottoman Empire. This is evident by the fact that the Turkish leaders of Mistra sent a letter to Mousaga telling him that Zaharias will be joining the operation and to kill him when the opportunity arrives. However, before the messengers could arrive in Dafni to give the letter to Mousaga, they were met by a few of Zaharias men who were guarding the Rasina River near Dafni. These men of Zaharias innocently proclaimed that they were men of Mousaga and that they were on their way to see him. When the messengers mentioned that they have a letter to give to Mousaga, the men of Zaharias offered to take the letter from them and that they would personally give the letter to Mousaga. When it was agreed, the messengers handed over the letter to the men and returned back to Mistra. Zaharias received and read the letter, which was addressed to Mousaga, which stated that he (Mousaga) should find a way to somehow kill Zaharias.

Upon reading the message, Zaharias had to find a clever way to remain at a distance from Mousaga in order to deny him of any opportunity to carry out the orders by the Turkish leaders (in case any other messages had leaked through to Mousaga about killing Zaharias). But, at the same time, Zaharias also wanted to attack and capture Merakos. First, Zaharias made up a fictitious story to Mousaga saying that one of his men stole 100 louphedes from a priest and that he needed to round up all his men in order to be able to interrogate them at some secluded venue. He even brought a priest, from the region, to Mousaga to make it appear as if the story was true.

Zaharias rounded up his men and separated his unit from Mousaga. With this in place, Zaharias succeeded in denying Mousaga of any opportunity in carrying out the Turkish leaders wishes. After this, the second tactic that Zaharias used was to tell Mousaga that he (Zaharias) and his klephtes would attack Merakos with the condition that Mousaga and his unit withdraw from the battlefield. This second tactic was basically a security matter, by having Mousaga and his unit, withdraw from the battle-field posed less of a threat for Zaharias and his men. When the condition was agreed, Zaharias started his attack on Merakos and Avdi.

As Zaharias was approaching the fort, he ordered his "engineers" who were from the village of Kosma (located in the Parnon mountains of the Kynoria region of Arcadia), to construct an underground tunnel that would lead right up to the fort. Kosma was known for housing "engineers" whose expertise was building not only underground tunnels but other architectural projects as well. The advancement of Zaharias, made it easier for his "engineers" to dig and construct the underground tunnel all the way to the fort of Merakos. Once completed, the "engineers" placed explosives under the fort, which had the result of knocking down one of the walls, thus enabling Zaharias and his men to enter the fort and capture Merakos and his rebels. It should be mentioned that this tactic was also used by Kolokotronis in the Greek War of Independence of 1821 when he captured the city of Tripoli.

The total number of rebels captured by Zaharias was 48, which also included Merakos and Avdi. Out of the 48 rebels, 36 were Turkish and 12 were Greek. It is uncertain how many of these rebels were killed in battle and how many died from the explosion of the fort. Zaharias ordered his men to cut the heads off Merakos and Avdi along with all of the Turkish rebels, while at the same time, the lives of the 12 Greek rebels of Merakos were spared and were consolidated into Zaharias unit. All of the Turkish heads that were cut off were sent to the Turkish Pasha of Tripoli. The events involving the military operation against Merakos occurred in February 1787.

Despite the fact that Zaharias was able to defeat and execute Merakos and his rebel unit, the Turkish Pasha of Tripoli (Vizer) was still displeased. The reason being was that Zaharias executed and sent only the heads of Merakos, Avdi, and the rest of the Turkish rebels to the Pasha in Tripoli, and not the Greeks who were fighting for Merakos. The following letter from the Turkish Pasha to Zaharias is evidence of this: "Kapetan Zaharias, Dervenagas of the Peloponnese. You sent the heads of the rebels and Merakos, and I am grateful, but the Greek heads you did not send me." Zaharias replied in the following manner: "Veziri, (Vizer) Pasha (of the Peloponnese). The Turks are yours (for judgement). The Greeks are mine, and I will judge them by the Greek laws, and do not cross me." Zaharias is making it clear to the Turkish ruler of the Peloponnese, that he wants to assume the role of judge and decide on cases involving his own Greek people. The Greek laws that Zaharias mentions in his reply to the Vizer, which were to be used as a basis for passing judgement, was none other than the "Armenopoulo" laws used in the old Byzantine Empire. The reply letter by Zaharias, infuriated, and at the same time, disappointed the Turkish Pasha of the Peloponnese.

The Vizer's greatest fears were now coming true, in that with Zaharias stating that he will assume responsibility of carrying out judgement on the Greek people, Vizer would lose control and influence over the Greeks, which the end result would be a loss of power in his jurisdiction (Peloponnese).

Since the Vizer's position and power was being threatened both politically and militarily, he decided to act by planning to do battle against Zaharias. He recognized the importance of acting swiftly and decisively in the circumstance that he was in, before it was too late. He decided to contact the well known Nikolopoulos family from Logastra, and offer them the title of Dervenagas, which Zaharias had already been appointed to, along with the monetary compensation that came with the title, should they fight and defeat Zaharias.

Zaharias was related with the Nikolopoulos family by marriage (as mentioned he married Pagona who was a relative of the Nikolopoulos family), and they had fought alongside together in the military operation against Merakos. The Turkish Pasha wanted to use this internal conflict between the two families to his advantage. Again, the Turks are implementing their well-known policy, called divide and conquer, to go after their enemies.

The Nikolopoulos family did go against Zaharias, but they later wanted to seek peace, while at the same time, Zaharias knew how important it was to end this senseless feud. They agreed to a peaceful end to the conflict, and Zaharias forgave the Nikolopoulos family for what they tried to do to him. Zaharias forgiveness, comes as no surprise since it was part of his nature and personality to forgive his enemies if they should ask for it. As part of their pact, and new found friendship and trust, Zaharias and Andonis Nikolopoulos, who was the patriarchal family leader, decided to arrange a marriage in the future between Zaharias daughter, Katerina, and Adonis Nikolopoulos's son Nikolas. Thus, both families decided to forget the past and start over with a clean slate. With the agreement in place, the Nikolopoulos family became a trusted and competent ally of Zaharias, in which they were always ready to support him, in order to fight the Turks when needed.

Zaharias sent a letter to the Vizer, in which he stated that he wanted to challenge him to battle. The letter to the Vizer was as follows: "You used all of your lies with the Nikolopoulos. I now want to do battle (against you) in the Imblakika region. Either you or I, this is my desire. Either blood, liberty or death!" The Imblakika region includes the southern part of Arcadia (directly south from the city of Megalopolis) along with the eastern half of Messinia. Zaharias wanted to set up a battle against the Vizer on his terms. He wanted to dictate the time of the battle, which was now, the place, which was the Imblakika region, and what was at stake. By doing this, Zaharias would have the advantage against the Vizer, since he would lure him to fight on his grounds. It was clear that what was at stake for Zaharias was not only the Dervenagas title, which he had, but also his power throughout the Peloponnese and, most likely, his own life.

The total number of fighting men that Zaharias had amassed for this military operation in the Imblakika region was about 3,000. The breakdown of this force was as follows: 400 men were from the unit of Zaharias, 600 from Mani, 1,300 Albanians, and 700 other men embarked on ships heading for the shores of Arcadia. Some historians believe that there were only about 100 men, which embarked on ships from the town of Bouka, and not the

700 mentioned by others. But in order for this operation to succeed for Zaharias, he had to have had a significant number of men on those ships. The naval operation with would have no chance of succeeding with a small force because one of the goals of this operation was to show to the Turkish officials and the Vizer, that there was another strong klephtic unit which was at the gates of Tripoli. By doing this, Zaharias was hoping to put much fear to the Turks, which would work to his advantage. Therefore, a unit of about 700 men on ships, seems like a likely figure for this particular task.

Overall, Zaharias had a very well thought out plan for the expected upcoming battle against the Vizer and the Turks. He wanted to lure the Turkish Pasha away from his home base of Tripoli and battle against him head on. At the same time, the klephtic rebels throughout the Peloponnese would revolt in their respected regions, so as to prevent any military assistance to the Vizer should he ask for it. Also, because of a Turkish decree, which was passed around this time, stating to arrest and / or kill the Albanians, Zaharias decided to incorporate them in his unit, in order that they may also fight the Turks. Zaharias knew how well the Albanians fought, and how aggressive they can be, in which by incorporating them into his unit, he would have another advantage over the Vizer. Most Albanians had a tendency to side with the Turks and fight against the Greeks because of the fact that they had the same religion. But with this new decree, the Albanians were put in a grave situation, which created an opportunity for Zaharias to incorporate them in his unit, since he had known that they would be fighting for their freedom as well. In addition, by sending the Maniates to Arcadia for a special mission, Zaharias was hoping to deceive the Vizer into thinking that a large klephtic unit was at the gates of Tripoli, thus putting much fear and panic to the Turks everywhere. Since the main Turkish forces would have left Tripoli with the Vizer, in order to do battle against Zaharias, the city would be left almost unprotected and vulnerable to any outside attack.

The Turkish Pasha (the Vizer), assembled his military forces and marched to the Imblakika region to a place called Tsakonia (not to be confused with Tsakonia of the Kynoria region of Arcadia), which is located across from Agrilovouni. The number of forces that he had assembled for this particular battle is estimated to be around 8,000. He must have had men with him spanning from all branches of his armed forces, except navel. He always had at his disposal a sizable force for the fact that he was the leader and governor of the Peloponnese reporting to the Sultan of the Ottoman Empire, and also he was based in a city that was always heavily fortified with a strong military presence.

The battle of Agrilovouni took place in the early summer of 1787. The actual battle started on a Wednesday, in which the Vizer ordered his men to attack. As his foot soldiers and cavalry were charging at the position held by their enemy, the Albanians serving under Zaharias opened fire with incredible accuracy, while at the same time, Zaharias ordered his men to concentrate mostly at firing at the Turkish cavalry. By shooting at the cavalry, Zaharias was hoping that this would slow down the advancement of the Turks.

By the end of the third day of the battle of Agrilovouni (Friday), as many as 200 Turkish cavalry were killed in action. With all that fighting, the Vizer had nothing to show for it, and at the same time, the morale of his troops had reached nearly rock bottom. At one point, the Vizer saw with his binoculars how the Maniates and Albanians were singing and dancing in celebration for being able to beat back the Turks. In addition, the Maniates also had the tendency to yell out wild war cries, which put much fear to their enemies. The Vizer held a meeting with his subordinates that Friday evening as to decide on what course of action they should take next. The decision they came up with was to attack Zaharias and his men on Saturday morning.

Kapetan Zaharias was also able to defeat the Turks decisively on Saturday morning. It is estimated that as many as 1,600 of the Vizer's troops were killed. After the Vizer's major defeat, he decided to send a message to all the regions of the Peloponnese (governed by his Turkish subordinates) asking them for military assistance, such as troops, supplies, and even canons, in order to fight and defeat Zaharias. But his subordinates from all of the regions of the Peloponnese responded back to him, saying that they could not offer any military assistance because they are being tied down by revolts from the klephtes. The revolt by the klephtes was part of Zaharias plan, mentioned above, which was outlined in the letters to Kolokotronis, Petimazas and the other captains from the Peloponnese. This strategy was not unusual for the klephtes, since it was part of the bylaws of the federation when it was formed in 1785. This was their way of how to combat the Turkish aggressors, which in the end proved very effective.

The Vizer decided to retreat back to Tripoli with the hope of defending the city from Zaharias. The military strategic position for the Vizer was not at all looking well for him. Three reasons why this was the case: First, he was not winning the battle in Agrilovouni. Second, there was another klephtic unit, which was threatening Tripoli. Third, the same unit that was threatening Tripoli, was also threatening the Vizer's rear position.

Seeing that the Vizer and the Turks were retreating, Zaharias yelled out to his men to get ready to attack at their enemy and chase them back to Tripoli. In addition to chasing after the Turks, Zaharias communicated to his men that they should also go after and take their possessions and military supplies from the battlefield and within the Turkish camps.

With this, Zaharias established another major victory against the Vizer and the Turks. It was a battle that lasted for nearly seven days, with many casualties suffered by the Turkish side. The actual battle site would later be named "kokkala" (in Greek it means bones), and this is because of the fact that there were so many Turks that lost their lives with this particular battle.

After his humiliating defeat in the battle of Agrilovouni, the Vizer held a major meeting in Tripoli to discuss what appropriate action to take. The meeting was attended by the Vizer's representatives and officials from the entire Peloponnese. They decided to send a letter to the Turkish Sultan of Constantinople. In this letter, they stated that there are many rebels in the Peloponnese and that Zaharias is a good and trustworthy person who is capable of going after them. In addition, they requested that the Sultan send a written decree in the form of a ferman which would give the right and authority for Zacharias to go after these rebels and be compensated via a portion of the tax revenues collected by the Ottoman Empire. A Turkish ferman is basically an order or permit granted by the Ottoman government giving exclusive rights or permission to an individual or group of people.

Basically what the ferman stated was that it not only reassured Zaharias his position as Dervenagas, but it also appointed him as "First Dervenagas" and Basbouglin. The title of Basbouglin was something that was given to the Beys or noble lords of Mani. Since now that Zaharias had relocated to the Mani region, the Turks decided to make him a Basbouglin, which gave the right to govern the area. In addition to all of the rights and privileges he received the first time he was appointed Dervenagas, Zaharias received even more this time around – hence the new title "First Dervenagas." His additional privileges gave him the right to collect taxes from any part of the Peloponnese as he sees fit and that he was the number one man in charge of security and policing the entire region. With this new recognition, especially coming from the Turkish Sultan of the Ottoman Empire, it solidified the recognition and position of the klephto-armatoloi federation, organized by Zaharias, in the Peloponnese society.

Zaharias sent letters and messengers to all of the captains and his subordinates throughout the Peloponnese announcing that he received a ferman from the Turkish Sultan and that he will be collecting and receiving money, which he will equally distribute to all of them. He also mentioned to them that they should stay put where they are, to be non-violent and to oversee the tranquility of their respected regions. Finally, he stated that they all must remain calm until the time is right to rise up and start a revolution for the sake of the Greek people. Zaharias knew very well that with so many battles in such a small time span, that the regions need it a break. But for him, this would be a temporary condition, the same way he knew that his new titles and positions would also be temporary, since his main goal is to free the land and the people from the Turkish yoke. This task can only be done through war and a revolutionary uprising by the people and the Greek rebels. He will try to use his "new found" status as one way of accomplishing his mission.

The next major event, which occurred in the life of Kapetan Zaharias, happened in July 1792. During this time, the war between Russian and the Ottoman Empire had ended, and the Turks were conducting "mopping up" operations throughout the Aegean Sea, in which they went after Greek ships that had not ended hostilities even after the treaty was signed. The man who led the naval warfare against the Turks was Lambros Katsonis, whose ships had sailed under the flag of the Russian Empire. Katsonis was still fighting the war at sea against the Turks with some success, even though military assistance from Russia had ceased. Along on this naval campaign was a well known klepht leader from Central Greece (Roumeli) named Kapetan Androutsos, who was the father of Odysseus Androutsos, hero of the Greek War of Independence of 1821. It is believed that Androutsos had a few hundred men with him on the ships of Katsonis.

The ships of Katsonis reached the shores of the southern tip of Mani near Porto Kagio. Androutsos and his men disembarked from the ships and went on land in order to seek help from Zaharias, who was in control of the region. Zaharias went out to meet Androutsos, and he invited him and his men to his fort in Skoufomiti, where they stayed for about six days. During his stay, Androutsos complained to Zaharias that he was being chased by the Turks and needed to go back to his home region safely. Zaharias promised that he would help his new friend to safe passage across the Peloponnese and into Central Greece (Roumeli).

Before setting out from Skoufomiti, careful preparations were made for this great and risky campaign. Zaharias ordered all of the Greek rebels for assistance, either by fighting the Turks in their respected regions, or by sending troops to unite with the forces of Zaharias and Androutsos. From Skoufomiti they battled their way up Laconia to Varvitsa, where they were received like heroes. After Varvitsa, they set out into Arcadia, and up the Peloponnese, marching in three different flanks. The right flank was to set out for the city of Corinth, located in the Northeast Peloponnese, so that they can prevent and cut off any Turkish attacks from the East and the Aegean Sea. The other two flanks were to march towards the Northcentral part of the Peloponnese near the town of Egio, where Androutsos and his men would cross over into Roumeli.

Along the march to Egio, Zaharias and Androutsos fought many battles against the Turks. One battle that stands out, happened in the village of Valtetsi, where Zaharias showed everyone his greatness as a true warrior and a fierce fighter. As the Turks were approaching the village, Zaharias picked 40 elite men and led the charge at the Turks, slaying many during the process and causing them to retreat in panic. Another battle, which again Zaharias showed his great military fighting skills, occurred in the village of Dara. It must be noted that Androutsos also proved to be a great fighter, in which he had already been known as the "lion of Roumeli."

After 40 days and nights from when they first started out at Skoufomiti, Zaharias and Androutos finally reached the town of Egio. Out of the 6,000 Turks who took part in the battles against the Greek rebels, nearly 1,500 lost their lives. Zaharias and Androutosos lost about 96 of their men. This military campaign truly proved to be very costly for the Turks in the Peloponnese. The Greeks had endured many hardships and obstacles throughout the 40 days. Theodoros Kolokotronis, who took part in the right flank for the Greek rebels marching towards Corinth, mentions that for a period of 15 days, they hardly ate or slept, but were fighting constantly.

The most significant thing that came out of this military campaign between Zaharias and Androutsos, other than the success of the operation, was the unity and bond of the two Greek klephtic forces. Zaharias told Androutsos that they should remain united and to hold on to his ideas. Also, that they should have an ongoing correspondence between them and that if he receives any money from the Turkish authorities (as an armatol) he should "spread the wealth" with the other Kapetans and rebel forces in his region. In addition, Zaharias mentioned to Androutsos of his desire to ask for military assistance from France in the hopes for planning the freedom for Greece. Should a revolution begin in the Peloponnese, which was the most likely case, Zaharias knew that Roumeli would play a vital role in that they would help prevent any Turkish forces from entering the Peloponnese. One sees how the unity between Zaharias and Androutsos was not just military but political as well. The unity was for a common

51

cause, the cause for freedom of the Greek people and for Greece.

After Zaharias returned from the town of Egio he started to plan for a naval operation against the Turks in the island of Egina. The reason for this operation was that Zaharias promised Androutsos that he would avenge to what happened to him a few months prior on that island. Androutsos had suffered severely against the Turks, forcing him off the island and ended up going with Lambros Katsonis. Zaharias set out for Egina with a total of 36 ships, which were mostly from Mani while some of the other ships had come from the Greek islands near the Peloponnese, such as Spetses. They arrived in Egina, where they made a surprise attack against the local Turkish authorities. The attack by Zaharias and his forces was concentrated only against the Turks and they were careful not to harm the Greeks living on the island. Zaharias and his men attacked and plundered the Turks, taking away their money and possessions.

When Zaharias returned back from the island of Egina, he sent some of the money to Androutsos and told him that he kept his word and avenged the disgrace he suffered. Androutsos was very pleased. The rest of the wealth Zaharias divided it up among the other rebel units in the Peloponnese. These latest attacks alarmed the Turks very much, in which they sent out another ferman to Zaharias reaffirming his authority and giving him money (louphedes) in the hopes of pacifying him. In addition, the Patriarch of the Greek Orthodox Church in Constantinople was also asked to send a letter to Zaharias to establish some sort of tranquility and calm in the region.

In 1794, a brutal crime occurred in the village of Kosma, located on the Parnon Mountains in the Kynoria region of the prefecture of Arcadia. A Turkish notable from Monemvasia named Alibey, passed through Kosma along with his entourage. He met this young beautiful Greek woman from the village, in which he tried every way possible to seduce her. He offered her money, jewelry and a good life if she agreed to become his wife and be part of his harem. However, she rejected all of Alibey's offers and advances. Because of this Alibey was angered and ordered his aides to grab the Greek woman, strip her naked and to cut off her breasts. The orders were carried out, and this young innocent Greek woman suffered a horrible death.

Zaharias was told of this terrible act in Kosma and he also found out that Alibey was making his way back to Monemvasia. He rounded up a small force, and with lightning speed he marched down to the road leading to Monemvasia in the hopes that he would be able to cut off Alibey before reaching his destination. Zaharias set up an ambush for Alibey, and as he was approaching the trap, Zaharias ordered the attack, in which he personally took out his sword and killed Alibey by cutting him to pieces. The entourage of Alibey was left unharmed and was allowed to return to Monemvasia. The cut up body of Alibey was sent to the Turkish authorities in Monemvasia with a message that read something to the effect that this is what happens to the Ottoman Turks who abuse the honor and religion of the Christians.

Kapetan Androutsos was captured by the Venetians and handed over to the Turks, in which they imprisoned him in Constantinople. In 1797, the Turks decided to execute Androutsos and dump the body in the Bosphorus Sea. Zaharias had lost a trusted friend and a comrade who shared in his view and passion about unity and freeing Greece from the Turkish yoke. Androutsos played a major role for the rebel forces in Central Greece. Meanwhile, the plans and dreams that Zaharias had in getting aid from France in order to start a revolution, which will lead to the freedom of Greece, suffered a temporary setback.

Between 1799 to 1803, there were two types of internal conflict that existed in the Peloponnese. On the one hand, the Greek rebels would battle Turkish forces in various regions throughout Southern Greece. And on the other, different factions of Greek rebels would fight against each other in the Mani region of Laconia. This was a time when Napoleon Bonaparte of France was storming through Europe and battling the major European nations both on the continent and beyond. Thus, the major European powers had a national interest in the Eastern Mediterranean and the Balkan region. With this in mind, the Turks were fearful that these major powers, especially France, would recruit the Greek rebels for the purpose of using them to cause havoc within the Ottoman Empire. Since the Greek Ionian Islands had come under the jurisdiction of France, the Turks viewed Napoleon as a greater threat to their Empire. Because of this, the Ottoman Empire decided to side with the European nations and go against Napoleon. This led to wide confrontations with the Greek klephtes, which resulted in little or no success at all.

The second type of conflict occurred mainly in the region of Mani. Greek klephtic units would fight against each other for reasons such as control of a certain area, power struggle, or because of a vendetta (family feud), which was very common among the family clans in Mani. The Greek klephtic units from various parts of the Peloponnese would head down to Mani in order to support and fight alongside their allies or friends as sort of a duty or loyalty to them. Even Zaharias and Kolokotronis were temporary fighting on opposite sides during this time period. According to the biography of Kolokotronis, he would fight against Zaharias, and at the end of every battle they would make amends and remain united. Its amazing to note that these two men remained united after each conflict and that the casualties suffered by the klephtes were very small and insignificant. Zaharias and Kolokotronis knew how important it was to be united, because without it the Greek klephtes would not be able to survive and the dream of liberation would never be realized.

Even during these internal conflicts, Zaharias would teach and educate the other Greek rebels on how to fight, and military tactics. He knew how vital it was for these rebels to sharpen their skills and to better prepare them for a future revolution and war of independence. But one cannot ignore the possibility that because of the internal conflicts, some of the other rebel groups remained bitter and refused reconciliation.

By mid 1803, Zaharias came up with the idea of having a correspondence with France and Napoleon in order to secure a military assistance from them, which would have the end result of liberating Greece. This was an era of revolution and nationalism that had taken the world by storm. Zaharias was no exception in taken wind of this, and he knew very well the important role that a major foreign nation would play in Greek affairs. He also knew that the Greek people needed the aid and support from a major foreign nation (in this case France) so that they would be able to withstand a prolonged revolution and have a greater chance of succeeding. The world was changing, and Zaharias wanted to capitalize on the opportunity of trying to liberate the Greek people. It must also be noted that during this period of 1803, Serbia started their own war of independence against the Ottoman Empire.

Zaharias did indeed correspond with Napoleon Bonaparte of France. Napoleon sent the Stephanopoulos brothers to Mani, to get intelligence information and to analyze the area. After finding the region ripe for a revolution, Napoleon sent a military ship (to meet up with Zaharias) named "Arab" to the town of Kitries, located in Mani, in September 1803. The ship unloaded military supplies and Zaharias invited the Captain and the crew of "Arab" to eat and drink together. In addition, Zaharias was handed a letter from Napoleon, which basically stated his support for a proposed revolution and outlined military plans for the near future uprising.

Zaharias had other well-known supporters in the Mani region, such as Tzanetbey from Gytheio, who was pro-French and had desires for an uprising. After the shipment, Napoleon started causing more problems for the Ottoman Empire. Naturally, the Turks and their supporters in the Peloponnese were very much alarmed and afraid by the developments and the possibility of a planned uprising. The plan by Zaharias was to start a revolution in the Mani region and from their have it spread to the entire Peloponnese, thereby liberating the Greeks living in Southern Greece. From there, Zaharias believed the revolution should spill over into Roumeli and beyond liberating towns and villages, while at the same time, freeing the Greek people.

The local Turks along with their Greek supporters informed the Vizer in Tripoli about the planned revolution by Zaharias. The Vizer received a ferman from Constantinople with orders to intervene and prevent any revolution from happening, while at the same time, they should capture and take Zaharias alive. Upon reading the orders from the ferman, the Vizer and his administration knew the difficult task bestowed on them in trying to capture Zaharias alive. The orders were trickled down to Antonbey Gregorakis, who was the governor of the Mani region, and was delegated the task of capturing Zaharias. This all occurred in October of 1803.

Zaharias had caused major headaches for the Turks in the Peloponnese throughout his entire life. But now he was becoming more uncontrollable, and ambitious with his plans in organizing an uprising to start a revolution. The Turks had to get Zaharias out of the way, in which they knew that this would be a difficult and dangerous mission. They could not simply round up troops and go after Zaharias or even attack him in an open pitch battle. They had tried this many times in the past, only to consistently fail on each occasion. A clever plan was needed to better assure the success of the mission. They decided on betrayal, either through a friend or relative, would be the best possible way to get rid of Zaharias and spoil any plans for an uprising.

The scope of the book is not to give a full detail analysis of the assassination of Zaharias. Rather, the focus here is to inform the readers on what happened and how this tragic event took place. The biggest debate by Greek historians is when did the assassination of Zaharias took place. The majority claim that it was in the year 1805 (October). The others say that it was on July of 1804, while a few insist on 1803. After a thorough examination, December 1803 seems like the most accurate date, which also agrees with non-Greek sources. Also, the close proximity between the time Zaharias received the shipment from Napoleon (September 1803) and his death (December 1803) makes sense. Another reason why it makes sense is that had Zaharias been killed in October of 1805 (two years later) the revolution would of already flared up and taken hold of the Peloponnese, which there is no evidence of this. The July 1804 date is confused with the assassination of Kapetan Petimazas of Kalavyta who, along with Kolokotronis, was second in command of the federation.

Antonbey Gregorakis now had the responsibility of carrying out the Turkish orders as stated in the ferman. The task rested on his shoulders and he knew that if he failed his life would be forfeited and the Turkish Vizer would cut off his head. Gregorakis assembled all of his supporters to plan out a way of capturing Zaharias. The plan had to be perfect, and they needed to find a trusted friend of Zaharias who would be persuaded in carrying out the grim task.

They found someone by the name of Koukeas who was from the outskirts of the town of Tseria, located in the northwestern part of Mani, in the prefecture of Messenia. Koukeas was indeed a trusted friend in which, one of his children had been baptized by

Zaharias. Antonbey Gregorakis and his allies promised Koukeas that if he betrayed Zaharias, he would receive considerable wealth and was even offered a position of authority within the government. The only catch was that he was asked that he should kill Zaharias and not to capture him alive as stated in the ferman. Koukeas had run into financial problems during this time, which is one reason why he was selected for the task because he would be the most likely candidate to accept. This tempting, but dangerous offer was accepted by Koukeas, and he immediately began making plans in order to carry out his mission.

Koukeas had sent a letter to Zaharias to come to Tseria in order to provide him with valuable information about the Turkish naval fleet anchored off the coast from the town of Kitries. Indeed, there was a Turkish naval fleet, which had blockaded the town of Kitries, since Zaharias received his military supplies there from Napoleon back in September. The blockade was put into effect to prevent any other ships with military supplies from reaching the harbor. Zaharias accepted the invitation to visit Koukeas.

Zaharias and his men first arrived at the Town Square in Tseria to attend a feast that was scheduled for that evening. During the feast, a nephew of Koukeas, named Martakos, joined Zaharias at his table, in which they started to converse about various issues. A little later, Zaharias and his two bodyguards left the party with Martakos to visit Koukeas. They arrived at the fort of Koukeas located just outside of the town of Tseria, in which both Zaharias and Martakos entered the residence, but the two bodyguards were left outside. It should be noted that in the Mani region, the family clans built forts made out of stones, which served not only as a place-of residence, but also as a fortress to defend against any enemy attack.

It is believed that once they were inside, both Zaharias and

Martakos went up the stairs to enter the upper level of the fort. Martakos opened the door, and allowed Zaharias to enter first. Once inside, Martakos shot Zaharias in the back and then proceeded in locking the door behind him. Zaharias was shot a few more times by Koukeas and his allies who were waiting for him inside. The bodyguards exchanged gunfire with the men inside the fort, and then decided to rush back to the Town Square to alert the others. The men of Zaharias fast tracked back to the fort where they were met by a sizable force and heavy resistance. They were too late, Zaharias had already been assassinated. The assassins found that Zaharias had on him a copy of a letter from Napoleon detailing the battle plans for a revolution. The great hero of Greece had been gone. Zaharias was dead, along with his dream (at least temporary) of liberation.

Koukeas took the head of Zaharias, which had been cut off, and went to the local Turkish authorities hoping to cash in on the rich reward that was promised to him. The Turks nabbed Koukeas were he was first mutilated and later executed for "killing such a great hero." The reasons why the Turks punished Koukeas was because they did not want to hold their end of the bargain and pay out the reward. In addition, they wanted to show the Greek population that they punished the man responsible for the death of their hero, Zaharias, so as to prevent any reprisals or revolts by the people.

Here is a sad song depicting the assassination of Zaharias:

> *Villages and towns did you hear?*
> *Did you also hear Varvitsiotes?*
> *Don't change for Easter, don't wear white.*
> *Like the rooster's (dark) wing, you should imitate.*
> *They killed Zaharias, in the fort of Koukeas.*
> *He was the flag of Mani and the pillar of the*
> *Peloponnese.*

*Where he was idolized in Tripoli, life the fresh spring
water.*
*As his associates heard the bad news, they started
dying one by one.*
And a young first cousin of Zaharias.
*Stands at an intersection of the road, admiring the
mountain peaks.*
*Have you seen your Kapetan?" (She asks to some
passing lads).*
*Why do you ask us? What do you want us to tell
you?*
He was shot ten times, with silver bullets.
There you will hear sadness and sorrow.
By the women of Mani who mourn their first Kapetan.

Thus, the life of Kapetan Zaharias, which had been so glorious,
ended in an inglorious way. It is interesting to note that future
owners of the fort of Koukeas changed the name to fort of
Zaharias. In addition, the area or village outside of Tseria, where
Zaharias was assassinated had also been changed to Zaharias in
the year 1960.

After the assassination of Zaharias, the klephto-armatoloi federation of the Peloponnese collapsed. With Zaharias out of the
way, the Turks seized the opportunity to go after the other rebel
leaders by using the same method of betrayal. One by one the
rebel leaders (along with the non-leaders) were being betrayed
and executed. Between 1804-1806 the Greek klephtes were constantly being persecuted throughout the Peloponnese.
Kolokotronis tried his best to rescue the situation and step up as
the leader of the Greek rebels. But his family and allies were
being executed around him, and at the same time, the Turks along
with their Greek supporters were chasing after him. Many of the
Greek klephtes were killed during this time period, while most
of them fled the Peloponnese for safety in the Ionian Islands,

which were under foreign control.

Zaharias was the most powerful klepht of his time in the Peloponnese. He was a true leader of the Greek rebels, who not only changed the thinking and attitude of the Greek klephtes, but also changed the history of Modern Greece. Eventually this change trickled down to the enslaved Greek people. The Turks had a famous saying about Zaharias, "ne gelde, ne gelchek," which means there never has been and there will never be another man like him. Zaharias fought against tyranny. He fought for liberation. He fought for freedom of the Greeks and the Greek lands. And he also fought for freedom of the future generations of Greeks. He was beloved by the poor Greeks, living under harsh conditions. Many songs were written and sung (even today) about him, his bravery, and his deeds. The Greek War of Independence began in 1821, and had Zaharias lived he would have been 62 years of age. Certainly he would have been the leader and general commander of the Greek armed forces leading the charge to victory and independence. But had Zaharias lived, the Greek War of Independence would probably of began a lot earlier than 1821.

Kapetan Zaharias – Commander in Chief of the Peloponnese.

View of the main peak of Skoufomiti from the "Halasmata tou Zaharia."

62

CHAPTER THREE

This chapter will cover some of the major events of the life history of Andonis Nikolopoulos, hero of the Greek War of Independence of 1821. Along with mentioning his life history, information will also be included on other members of the Nikolopoulos family.

The name Nikolopoulos came about when the two brothers, Andonis and Panagiotis, took their fathers' first name and made it their new last name. Their father's name was Nikolaos Palaios who was from the village of Pigadia, located in the northwestern part of Mani on the western side of the Taygetos Mountains. Nikolaos Palaios was a klepht, and when he became an adult, he settled in the village of Logastra (located on the Taygetos Mountains in Laconia) where he got married and started a family. Thus we can say that the roots of the Nikolopoulos family was from Pigadia, Mani. Eventually, Nikolaos Palaios would also be known as Nikolopoulos (or as Nikolaion) late in his life. The name Palaios most likely derives from the family dynasty of Palaiologos. After the fall of Constantinople and the collapse of the Byzantine Empire, this powerful family, in which many of them controlled the Peloponnese and were based in Mistra, scattered to the western and northwestern part of Mani (western side of the Taygetos Mountains). Their descendants branched out into different family clans, changing their family names several times throughout the centuries. The name Palaios is the shorter version or was cut from the name Palaiologos. The modifying or changing of last names became a common practice in Greece during this time period. It must be noted that it is also believed that prior to settling in Logastra, the Nikolopoulos family had come from the prefecture of Arcadia via Pigadia.

When did Nikolaos Palaios (Nikolopoulos) first settle in Logastra is uncertain. Most likely he probably first settled in the early 1740's from Pigadia when he was a young adult in his 20's. He married in Logastra and had two sons, the oldest named Panagiotis (1745?) and the younger one named Andonis born in 1748. Panagiotis was nicknamed "leikos" (wolf) because legend has it that a wolf attacked him while he was asleep, but Panagiotis managed to fight the wolf and strangle it to death. Both Panagiotis and Andonis were known for their bravery, strength and their mastery over weapons. But Andonis was also known for his intelligence and his ideas, which were far ahead of his time. He was a logical thinker and was regarded with great respect and admiration from others. So much so, that when the father, Nikolaos Palaios passed away at a very young age, it was Andonis who took over the family clan, and not his older brother Panagiotis.

It is uncertain exactly when Nikolaos Palaios died, but being that he was young and Andonis was of age to lead the Nikolopoulos family, it is more likely that his untimely death happened in the late 1770's. During this time period, Andonis married a woman belonging to the Simitaion family from the village of Tripi, located near Logastra in the Taygetos Mountains.

In 1775, the Turks and their Albanian allies were heading towards the region known as Outer Mani near the village of Pigadia to pillage and devastate the area. The Nikolopoulos family and there rebel unit, in an effort to prevent the destruction of the area, fought and defeated the Turks and their allies decisively. After this great victory, the Nikolopoulos family was not only recognized as the most powerful klephtic family in Laconia, but also the most respected and well known. They controlled a large vicinity within their region, which included not only Logastra and the surrounding areas of Mistra, but also Northern Laconia and down through Mount Taygetos, just south of the village of Anavriti.

The notoriety and recognition the Nikolopoulos family achieved was the main reason why Zaharias went to Logastra when he decided to become a klepht. As mentioned in the previous chapter, in 1776 Zaharias left Varvitsa for Logastra in the hopes of joining the klephtic organization that was based there. He had heard about the accomplishments of the Nikolopoulos family, and their well-fortified base, which was used as a training ground for the klephtic rebels. When Zaharias arrived in Logastra, he was able to join the rebel unit of Kapetan Matzari who was based there at the time and was with Nikolopoulos. They had very strict rules as to who can join their rebel force, like for example, they would not allow criminals or rapists to become members of their unit. The Nikolopoulos family had two forts in the Logastra vicinity. The first one was located outside of Logastra in the small village of Soustianous (located at a higher elevation) and was used to defend any attacks against the Turks. A second fort, which was better fortified than the first, was located in the municipality of Kastoriou (Taygetos Mountains) and was used as a training facility for the rebels and potential officers from the prefecture of Laconia. This second fort was also known as "the base of Nikolopoulos."

Since the Nikolopoulos family had become the most powerful klephtic family in Laconia, it very likely that they had ties and correspondence with other powerful klephtic families in the Peloponnese, such as the Kolokotonis family from Arcadia and the Panagiotaros family from Mani. Logastra is near the Laconian-Arcadian border, so it was natural for Nikolopoulos to be in close touch with the Kolokotronis family, who were bouncing around all over the place. Theodoros Kolokotronis (hero and leader of the Greek War of Independence), mentions of the close bond between the two families. With the Panagiotaros family, there must have also been an alliance and a close bond. The Nikolopoulos family ventured out to their roots in Pigadia, located in Outer Mani. Because of this, they benefited from having an alliance with the most powerful family in Mani, led by Panagiotaros Venetsenakis. Also, Zaharias and his father knew Panagiotaros very well, so a connection between the two very powerful families can be made through Zaharias. By having this bond and correspondence, they shared their experiences and warfare, which was advantageous for the Greek rebels.

When the Turkish naval commander Hasan Tzetzarli was sent to the Peloponnese in 1779 to get rid of the Albanians and bring order to the region, the Nikolopoulos family was involved in this operation. The Turks had decided to form an alliance with the Greek klephtes of the Peloponnese, to unite their efforts and pool their resources in going against the Albanians. Since they were the most powerful klephtes in Laconia, and at the same time, Constantine Kolokotronis was leading the Greek rebels in this mission, its only logical that they should set the example and support the military campaign. The Albanians were decisively defeated, and the Nikolopoulos family played a significant role in this victory and in leading the Laconian klephtes.

After the "Albanian operation" was completed, the Turks demanded the Greek klephtes to submit and pay their respect to the government authorities in order to attain amnesty. The Nikolopoulos family along with a few other klephtes refused this demand. In July 1780, the Turks laid siege the forts of Kastania in Mani, which was gallantly defended by the forces of Panagiotaros and Kolokotronis. In the end, the Greek klephtes could not hold the forts in Kastania, and were soundly defeated by the Turks. There is no evidence that the Nikolopoulos family took part in this tragic battle against the Turks. However, it is

66

possible that some of their members or even some of the klephtes they had trained in Logastra, took part in defending the forts in Kastania against the Turkish attacks.

During the time period of 1780-81, the Turks had set out to try to subdue the Maniotes and the Mani region. Mani had always enjoyed being autonomous and the Maniotes were very warlike and independent from the Ottoman Empire. In addition, Mani was used as a safe haven for klephtes who were on the run or being chased by their enemies. Another force consisting of Turks and Greeks, who agreed to the demands of the Turkish authorities in exchange for amnesty, marched to Mani with an objective to subdue the Maniates and control the region. As they entered the Mani region, they were attacked by a force of Greek klephtes, led by the Nikolopoulos family. Around this time period, the Nikolopoulos family was not only in charge of the klephtes in their home prefecture of Laconia, but they also commanded the klephtes from the prefecture of Messenia as well. The Nikolopoulos and the klephtes went to fight the Turks and their Greek allies in order to defend the Mani region. The battle took place in the area known as Almiro, located in the northwestern part of Mani in the prefecture of Messenia. After fierce fighting, both sides decided to hold a dialogue and possibly come to a peaceful resolution. But Nikolopoulos and his klephtes had a clever plan in mind. Their plan was to kill the Greek leaders who had sided with the Turks as they were conducting the dialogue. During the dialogue proceedings, they opened fire and manage to kill a few pro-Turkish Greek leaders, including the flag bearer. The Turks and their Greek allies fled the area, and the Nikolopoulos family, along with their rebel force, was victorious. The Nikolopoulos family was not only fighting against the Turks and their allies, but they were also fighting for their old homeland, since Almiro is near the village of Pigadia, where they originally came from.

After the great victory for Kapetan Zaharias in the battle of Salesi (1781), the family Nikolopoulos came to congratulate Zaharias and they made an oath to him in which they pledged their full support and that they would bring anything he needed from their region of Logastra-Mistra. Zaharias told them that he needed led (bullets), gunpowder, stones, and leather shoes. In addition, he told them that money and bread he can get with his sword.

Since they believed in Zaharias and that they saw in him a young, charismatic, brave and strong warrior, with great insight and a future leader, the Nikolopoulos family offered to marry one of their relatives, named Pagona, to him. Zaharias accepted the offer and the arranged marriage took place in the year 1782. Arranged marriage was a mainstream practice. Sometimes it was used to bond two powerful families, or to seal some sort of agreement. But there were also other reasons why this practice took place. In this particular case, the Nikolopoulos family was well known and powerful in Laconia, while at the same time, Zaharias was quickly becoming powerful, respected and feared by the Turks. In addition, since their home village of Logastra is in close proximity of Mistra and Tripoli, two major cities with a large Turkish force, the Nikolopoulos family was constantly sought after by their enemies. Therefore, they needed to build a network alliance and make allies in order to survive and defend against the Turks and their supporters. Thus, Zaharias was the most obvious choice and the perfect match.

Problems did indeed develop between the Turks and the Nikolopoulos family. It seems as though they were being harassed and chased by the Turks. This prompted Zaharias to write a letter to the local Greek "political leaders" of Sparta - Mistra (these so called "political leaders" worked for their local Turkish bosses) in which their names were Krevvatas and Kopanitsas, respectively. In the letter he basically mentions that since he is now a relative of the Nikolopoulos family, he wants the local chief of security of Mistra to stop chasing them. Zaharias wanted to defend and protect the Nikolopoulos family (his in-laws) from any danger or threat. He stayed in the villages of Xerovouna and Logastra for a short time before returning back to Varvitsa.

In 1785, Kapetan Zaharias formed a klephto-armatoloi federation for the main purpose of uniting all of the Greek rebels in the Peloponnese in order to liberate the enslaved Greek people from the Turkish yoke. The federation had other objectives, including achieving armatoloi status (similar to what existed in Central Greece) and being compensated by the Turkish and their Greek supporters in the Peloponnese for the protection and security of the land. The Nikolopoulos joined and were members of the federation, in which for many years they were compensated by the Turks and the Greek Kotsabasides to oversee and protect the land and properties in their respected regions. In addition, the commander-in-chief of the federation, Kapetan Zaharias, would send money to the Nikolopoulos (and to other klephtes) as monetary assistance for their expenditures. As mentioned above, the Nikolopoulos family was harassed by the Turks and Zaharias came to their defense. The formation of the federation was one of the greatest ideas by Zaharias because it not only served to protect the Nikolopoulos from any harassment or injustice, but also to safeguard other klephtes.

Zaharias, Nikolopoulos, Kolokotronis and other klephtes became heroes and were idolized by the enslaved Greek people. Many poems and songs were written and song by the people to honor and celebrate their heroism and bravery. The following song relates to this and was well known not only in the Peloponnese, but also in the Greek Ionian Islands who heard about their accomplishments:

> *Nikolopoulos (family) you're amazing——And*
> *Karaggiozis fights,*

See how Zaharias annihilates the Turks,
So that they may save the generation——To
everyone's delight.
Chresantakis, Yiannias, Tzavaras, and Tsamalis,
See Kolokotronis——How many of the enemy he
kills,
They run like beasts——Delighted with fire.

In 1787, Zaharias was given the title of Dervenagas (see previous chapter), and he went after the Turkish-Albanian outlaw named Merakos and his followers. The Turks had tried for months to capture Merakos, but were unsuccessful. The Nikolopoulos family and there klephtic unit joined Kapetan Zaharias in this military operation. They knew that this would be a major military operation and not a simple task, in that, Merakos was not only a fierce fighter, but also was very well fortified in the village of Dafni, Laconia. Zaharias, however, was able to blow up the fort and defeat Merakos, who was killed, along with his supporters. The supporters of Merakos who were not of Greek descent and were able to survive the battle, were executed by Zaharias.

It was because Zaharias decided to execute the captured non-Greek outlaws and incorporate into his own unit the captured Greek outlaws, that upset the Turkish Pasha, or Vizer, of the Peloponnese. Other than the fact that he will not receive the heads of the Greek outlaws, another reason why the Turkish Vizer was upset with Zaharias, was that he was now seen as an even greater threat with the possibility of causing military and political instability in the Peloponnese. By Zaharias carrying out judgement on the Greek people, the Vizer would lose control and influence over the Greeks, which the end result would be a loss of power in his jurisdiction (Peloponnese).

The Vizer recognized the importance of acting swiftly and decisively in the circumstance that he was in, before it was too late. He decided to contact the Nikolopoulos family from Logastra, and offer them the title of Dervenagas, which Zaharias had already been appointed to, along with the monetary compensation that came with the title, should they fight and defeat Zaharias. The Turks are implementing their well-known policy called divide and conquer, to go after their enemies. The Nikolopoulos family accepted the offer.

Zaharias had found out what was going on and of the planned attacks by Nikolopoulos. The Turks had sided with the Nikolopoulos family and had planned surprise attacks on Zaharias and his rebel force. But Zaharias was able to beat back the surprise attacks and put an end to this conflict. Thankfully, the hostilities ended very quickly and any chance of the internal conflict spreading within the federation ceased. The following song pertains to the bitter conflict and its peaceful resolution:

> Two flags came, not far from Mistra.
> The battle started, with muskets opening fire,
> They both take out their swords, Zaharias and Andonis (Nikolopoulos).
> They charged at each other, no one was killed.
> In (the count of) two, in three they yelled out to each other:
> Brothers, why do we fight, Greeks against Greeks;
> Let us go and kill the Turks, (and) the pashas.

After they realized the grave position that they were in, the Nikolopoulos family had to try to seek peace, while at the same time, Zaharias knew how important it was to end this senseless feud. They agreed to a peaceful end to the conflict, and Zaharias forgave the Nikolopoulos family for what they tried to do to him. Zaharias forgiveness, comes as to no surprise since it was part of his nature and personality to forgive his enemies if they

71

should ask for it. As part of their pact, and new found friendship and trust, Zaharias and Andonis Nikolopoulos, who was the patriarchal family leader, decided to arrange a marriage in the future between one of the daughters of Zaharias, Katerina, and Andonis Nikolopoulos's son Nikolas. Thus, both families decided to forget the past and start over with a clean slate. With the agreement in place, the Nikolopoulos family became a trusted and competent ally of Zaharias, in which they were always ready to support him, in order to fight the Turks when needed.

Between 1790-1792, there was a minor outbreak of an epidemic (similar to the plague) in the Balkans, which resulted in many people dying or being ill. The Peloponnese was hit the hardest out of all the regions in Greece. Sadly, it is believed that the wife of Kapetan Zaharias, Pagona, passed away during this time because of the epidemic. Zaharias would later marry again for the second time. Pagona, who was probably around 30 years old when she died, was a relative of the Nikolopoulos family.

As mentioned in the previous chapter, in the summer of 1792, Kapetan Androutsos of Roumeli passed through the Mani region, only to be helped by Kapetan Zaharias for safe passage back to his home region. It is uncertain if the Nikolopoulos family and their rebel forces participated in this heroic and glorious military campaign across the Peloponnese. But because Zaharias invited all of the klephtic forces throughout the Peloponnese to provide assistance in this matter, as part of the bylaws of the federation, the Nikolopoulos rebel force most likely took part and ventured in supporting the campaign. It is possible that as Zaharias and Androutsos were making their way to Varvitsa to get through Arcadia and the Central Peloponnese, the Nikolopoulos family participated alongside them in the campaign against the Turks.

The time period of 1799-1803, witnessed internal conflicts in the Mani region, involving different factions of Greek klephtic units and local powerful families. There is no evidence that the Nikolopoulos family was involved in this power struggle. The status quo had remained unchanged for the Nikolopoulos for several years, in which they were still well respected with a significant rebel force and based in Logastra. The only other information pertaining to the Nikolopoulos family during this time period, was their involvement in the real estate buying agreement of Zaharias. On February 10 1802, Zaharias bought some land in what is now the modern city of Sparti (family descendants still own it today). In the contract agreement of the property, Panagiotis Nikolopoulos signed as a witness to the sale agreement, which was made in his home village of Logastra. This shows the close bond between the families of Zaharias and Nikolopoulos since their reconciliation from the bitter feud some 15 years earlier.

After the assassination of Kapetan Zaharias in December 1803 and the collapse of the klephto-armatoloi federation, the Greek klephtes were persecuted by the Turks and their supporters. By the end of the persecution in the spring of 1806, many klephtes had lost their lives, while others fled the Peloponnese for the "safe venues" of the Ionian Islands. It is uncertain if any member of the Nikolopoulos family was killed, wounded, or escaped the turmoil of the Peloponnese during this period. However, evidence does indicate that at least some of its members, especially Andonis Nikolopoulos, stayed in the Peloponnese and were able to hide from the Turks during and after the persecution.

William Martin Leake was a British traveler, writer, military officer, and an expert in foreign affairs, traveled the Peloponnese during the time of the persecution of the klephtes. His task was to survey the area and gather intelligence information from the peninsula for Great Britain. Leake's personal experiences in the Peloponnese and the information he gathered was later published

73

in a book, which he wrote, titled "Travels in the Morea" (3 volumes, London 1830). The word Morea refers to the Peloponnese as it was known back then.

In his log, Leake indicates that on May 5 1805, he was planning to travel from the city of Kalamata, located in the prefecture of Messenia, to Mistra through the difficult and dangerous terrain of the Taygetos Mountains. These mountain passes were being held and controlled by the klephtes as a safe haven against enemy attack. From the mountains the klephtes can defend and attack or capture Turkish forces or government officials, who just so happen to be passing by. In addition, they would escort foreign visitors and locals to safe passage. This was one part of the klephtic way of life. Elias Tzanes, a high ranking Greek political representative (Kotsabasi) and a British agent, accompanied Leake to the Taygetos Mountains when they met Kapetan Andonis from Logastra, who assured them protection and safe passage through the mountains. Kapetan Andonis is none other than Andonis Nikolopoulos from Logastra. Leake, however, changed his mind and decided on an alternate route.

After the turmoil and hostilities against the klephtes ended in the Peloponnese and in the other parts of Greece, there was a period of calm and peace throughout the land. Except for some minor skirmishes and short lived conflicts, the years between mid 1806 to February 1821 experienced an unusual prolonged pacification, which was something not seen in many decades. There was however, a movement during this time to organize for the cause to liberate Greece. This movement was conducted and organized by the Greek Diaspora living abroad.

In 1814, a group of Greeks came together in Russia for a common purpose. They decided to form an organization or society, in which its mission would be to help support and organize a revolution to liberate the Greeks from the tyranny of the Otto-

74

man Empire. This organization was named Philiki Etairia (Friendly Society) and its members took an oath to pledge their allegiance to the society and its mission. The Philiki Etairia later relocated its headquarters to Constantinople in 1818 so as to reach out to more Greeks and increase the size of its membership. By the time the Greek War of Independence was about to begin, the membership was widespread throughout the land and had increased to a large and significant number. All of its members had secret names and communicated with each other in special code. They believed that the Greek War of Independence should begin in the Peloponnese.

It is uncertain when Andonis Nikolopoulos became a member of the Philiki Etairia, but he pledged his support for the cause and respected his duty for the organization. It is also uncertain if there were any other members of the Nikolopoulos family who joined the society. What is certain is that Andonis Nikolopoulos wanted to liberate Greece and fight for the Greek people. This was his life long dream and passion. He would get involved with anything that had to with the liberation, whether it would be warfare or not. He wanted to play a major role in the affairs of the Peloponnese and the war campaign against the Ottoman Empire.

In November 1820, Papaflessas, who was a member of the Philiki Etairia, arrived in the Peloponnese from Constantinople via the Greek Island of Hydra. His goal was to spread the message about the upcoming Greek revolution and to avoid any possible delays or obstacles. But he also had to organize for the revolution within the Peloponnese, which was one of the tasks of the Philiki Etairia. Since Papaflessas was originally from the village of Poliana in the Peloponnese, he knew many competent and well-respected individuals to hold discussions and carry out his mission. In his travels throughout the Peloponnese, he also went to Logastra to meet with Andonis Nikolopoulos, a fellow member of the Philiki

Etairia. They discussed the matter of organizing a Greek revolution against the Ottoman Empire and about the possibility of where and when it should begin. Nikolopoulos was very enthusiastic about the idea and he pledged his support for the cause of the revolution, which is also the cause for freedom.

Along with preparing and organizing militarily for the Greek revolution, Andonis Nikolopoulos also donated money to support the war cause. The amount of money donated is not certain, but it probably occurred around the time of Papaflessas' visit to Logastra. It is a known fact that with any campaign, be it political, military, or anything else, money and wealth play a major role in the running, and hopefully, achieving successful results. The Greek revolution needed funds from the beginning or else in would not take off from the ground. Without financial support, the military campaign would be doomed and the dreams for Greek liberation would vanish. Andonis Nikolopoulos was willing to support the cause any way he could, whether it be financial, or military.

The Greek War of Independence was pegged for March 1821. During this time, final preparations were being made for the "Herculean" task of liberation from the Turkish yoke. It was decided that the war should begin in the Peloponnese with the hopes that it would create a chain reaction to the other parts Greece, including the Greek Islands. Andonis Nikolopoulos became an officer of the Laconian revolutionary forces. He was one of the best leaders in Laconia, and was perfect for that position.

From March 11, the message had been passed along throughout the prefecture of Laconia, about the upcoming revolution. Meanwhile in Logastra, Andonis Nikolopoulos had gathered his forces and was making preparations to lay siege on the fort of Mistra. When the Turks in Mistra got word of the planned attack by the

Greeks, they decided to leave for their safety and head for the city of Tripoli in Arcadia. On March 20, they emptied out Mistra, and from the 15 thousand Turkish refugees, only 10 thousand were able to make it to Tripoli. With this act, the entire prefecture of Laconia became liberated from the Ottoman Empire. Laconia was the first province / prefecture to become liberated during the Greek War of Independence.

On March 28 1821, the newly liberated town of Mistra held an emotional church ceremony, with the presence of high ranking Greek officials and military officers, including Andonis Nikolopoulos and his unit of about three hundred men. They blessed the flag of the Greek revolution, and they all took an oath to fight for freedom.

From Mistra, Andonis Nikolopoulos went to the village of Vlachokerasia, located in the prefecture of Arcadia just south of Tripoli, to form a military base with a fellow officer, Kyriakoulis Mavromichalis from Mani. Nikolopoulos had with him about 300 men, while Mavromichalis had between 300-400 men, and the reason why they decided to form a base was so that they may attack the fortification of the city of Tripoli and its close proximity to the city.

Theodoros Kolokotronis sent a letter warning Nikolopoulos and Mavromichalis that they are in a grave strategic position in Vlachokerasia and that they should depart and join his base in Valtetsi (Arcadia). Mavromichalis replied back saying that they refuse to depart and if they should come under attack, Kolokotronis and his unit could come to the rescue.

In the pre-dawn hours of April 10, 1821, which also happened to be Greek Orthodox Easter Sunday, three thousand Turks from Tripoli, decided to make a surprise attack on the military camp of Vlachokerasia. The military camp in Vlachokerasia was divided up into two units, one under the command of Nikolopoulos, the other under Mavromichalis. Upon seeing the enemy, Mavromichalis and his men decided to leave the military camp, but Nikolopoulos stood his ground and prepared for battle. There were, however, a few men who belonged to the unit of Mavromichalis, but decided to stay behind and fight alongside the others. Nikolopoulos had many of his family members present in Vlachokerasia as part of his unit. The battle lasted between two to three hours and during the process, when all seemed lost, Nikolopoulos ordered many of his men to leave the battlefield for safety, but he decided to stay behind and fight on. When they ran out of ammunition, Nikolopoulos took out his sword and led a charge, killing the Turkish commander Hasanis Lestriotis. However, this gallant effort was short lived, in that Nikolopoulos was killed and the battle was over. In the end, 30 Turks were killed, 34 Greeks and 12 were taken as prisoners. Along with Nikolopoulos, another young officer was also killed in the battle, named Panagi Venetsenakis, nephew of Panagiotaros Venetsenakis who was killed by the Turks in 1780. The Turks beheaded all of the fallen Greeks and took the heads with them back to Tripoli. In addition, they also took the flags of Nikolopoulos, which consisted of a phoenix (rising bird out of ashes), a cross, the words "Liberty or Death" and the initials in Greek IXNK. The initials stood for "Jesus Christ Overcomes" (Ihsous Hristo Nika).

After the battle, the victorious Turks proceeded to burn the village of Vlachokerasia. The military base was destroyed and would no longer function for the entire duration of the war. The battle of Vlachokerasia was the first major battle of the Greek War of Independence. Also, Nikolopoulos was the first Greek military officer to be killed during the war. He was killed at the age of 73, fighting for his people and his country. The "old klepht" as he was often referred to, fought his entire life for liberty and was constantly battling the Turks and tyranny. This fallen hero, despite his age, never surrendered and kept on fighting even when all seemed to be lost. Kolokotonis mentioned that Nikolopoulos was a great leader.

Andonis Nikolopoulos had at least two sons, one named Nikolas, the other Demetris. It is not known how many other children he might have had. Both Nikolas and Demetris fought it many major battles during the war with honor and dignity. One battle that stands out happened in August 1825, when, alongside other Greeks, they battled the forces of Ibrahim Pasha between the villages of Silimnas and Davias, located near the city of Tripoli. Nikolas had the title of "Kapetan" for the Logastra-Mistra region. He married Katerina, daughter of Kapetan Zaharias. As mentioned above, the marriage of Nikolas and Katerina was agreed by their fathers in order to bring both families closer together and united.

In conclusion, Andonis Nikolopoulos was a true Greek hero, who fought and died for the independence of the Greek nation. For all of his klephtic life, he would constantly fight against Turkish tyranny and their supporters. He would create havoc for the Turkish authorities and would not give up the fight until victory was achieved or death. So much so that the Turks who were from the Bardounochoron region of the Peloponnese (north from the Mani region), and were regarded as one of the fiercest and bravest Turkish fighters, were very much afraid of Nikolopoulos, because of the many attacks he initiated against them. Nikolopoulos and his family set up military camps to train many Greeks and some even became great fighters and heroes and played a major role during the Greek War of Independence. With the battle of Vlachokerasia, Andonis Nikolopoulos will forever be immortalized in the pages of the Modern Greek History books. He and his 300 men courageously fought against an overwhelming Turkish force. He fought and died for freedom, just like the Ancient Spartan King Leonidas and his 300 men, who also fought and died for freedom fighting against King Xerxes and the Persians at Thermopolye. After the battle of Vlachokerasia, Greeks from all over came in droves to support the cause of liberation. It propelled other Greeks to take up arms and fight for freedom. This proves what a few brave men can accomplish if they fight tyranny and die for liberty.

On the left, Takis Nikolopoulos descendent of Antonis Nikolopoulos and on the right, Andrew Pagonis descendent of Kapetan Zaharias.

CHAPTER FOUR

This chapter will comprise of the history of Kapetan Petros Anagnostopoulos Barbitsiotis and the major role he played during the Greek War of Independence. To be consistent with the history time line, the name Anagnostopoulos will only be referred to up until the time Kapetan Petros was asked to change his name by Kolokotronis during the war. After that, the name Barbitsiotis will be used to refer to Kapetan Petros.

Petros Anagnostopoulos was born in 1785, in the village of Varvitsa, during the time when Kapetan Zaharias built his two forts and was becoming very powerful. His grandfather's name was Anastasios Soulimiotis, who was originally from the village of Soulima (now known as Upper Dorio) located in the prefecture of Messenia, and settled in Varvitsa around the 18th century. Soulimiotis was recognized as village president and leader of the klepht rebels coming out of Varvitsa. One of his sons was named Constantinos, who became involved with the church known as anagnostis. Constantinos had four sons and a daughter (grandchildren of Anastasios), named Petros, Demetris, Giorgakis, Nikolas and Martha, in which they all changed their last names to Anagnostopoulos, stemming from their father's involvement with church. Petros was the eldest of all the sons.

Petros Anagnostopoulos was a "pupil" of Kapetan Zaharias, in which he was able to learn from a very early age the finer points in fighting and military tactics. Since he was very close to Zaharias, he was able to pick up additional skills and showed much promise as a future leader. Most likely, he was probably admitted to the rebel unit of Zaharias between 1800-1802. Anagnostopoulos was able to escape persecution by the Turks and their allies, however he did not flee for the Greek Ionian Islands, like so many of his comrades. Instead, he decided to hide out and remain "invisible" until the outbreak of the Greek War of Independence of 1821. He also became a member of the Philiki Etairia and set his goals on liberating the Greek people.

As the threat of a Greek Revolution was becoming more of a reality, the Turks who were residing in the valley and coastline of Laconia, fled to Mistra for safety. During this time, Kapetan Petros was appointed as the leader of the Greek forces coming out of the Northern Parnon Mountains, known as Oinounda. Some time later, Kapetan Petros would become in charge of the Eastern Laconian forces. He and his men captured the abandoned town of Skoura, which formerly housed many Turkish families. But because the Turks in Mistra decided to pack up and flee to the city of Tripoli, Kapetan Petros had to leave from the village of Skoura, in order to handle the latest developments. However, he left behind a few of his men in Skoura so that they may protect the village and conduct various surveys.

From Skoura, Kapetan Petros went to the village of Vervena, located in the prefecture of Arcadia, where he became one of the original organizers in forming a military base there. The military base in Vervena was formed along with other well-known Greeks, who all became heroes of the Greek War of Independence. The reason for forming a military base was to counteract and pose a threat to the stronghold and important city of Tripoli, which was close by. This was around the time when the Greek War of Independence had just begun.

At the very start of the Greek Revolution, Kapetan Petros and his forces fought the Turks, who had come from Tripoli, in the villages of Frangovrisi and Kalogerovouni. As mentioned in the previous chapter, a Turkish force of three thousand attacked the Greek military base in Vlachokerasia led by Andonis Nikolopoulos and Kyriakoulis Mavromichalis. This was the first major battle in the Greek War of Independence and Andonis Nikolopoulos became the first Greek officer to be killed after refusing to retreat. The gunfire from the battle was heard all the way to Vervena, in which Kapetan Petros marched with his men to Vlachokerasia to provide assistance. When he arrived, the battle between Nikolopoulos and the Turks had already come to an end, but he still managed to attack the Turks, which resulted in a very lengthy battle. At the end of the battle, Kapetan Petros Anagnostopoulos lost 14 of his men. It should be noted that the remaining survivors from Vlachokerasia were incorporated into the military camp of Vervena.

On May 12-13, the Turks had attacked another Greek military base in Valtetsi (prefecture of Arcadia) not too far from Tripoli. Kapetan Petros arrived around midnight as reinforcement for the embattled Greeks. Since he realized that the other Greeks had been fighting for 16 consecutive hours and were exhausted from all the fighting, he decided to lead a charge and go through the enemy so as to make it to the other side and rescue the other Greeks who were there. He selected 17 good men, and with their swords in hand they made a sortie through enemy lines and successfully made it to the other Greek camp without a scratch. When they finally made it over to the other side, they were greeted there by Kyriakoulis Mavromichalis, commander of the Greek camp. Kapetan Petros and the 17 men brought along ammunition and other supplies. Mavromichalis mentioned to Kapetan Petros that their guns were ruined because of the rain and mud. In response to this, Kapetan Petros and his men opened fire and attacked the Turks (since their guns were dry), who retreated from the battlefield. Since more Greek reinforcements had arrived at the battle theatre, the Turks decided to pull out altogether from Valtetsi after 24 hours of fighting. This was a major victory for the Greeks and for the liberation movement.

The next battle, which involved Kapetan Petros was the battle of Vervena. On May 18, 6,000 Turks separated into three flanks quickly marched from their base in Tripoli to three different locations held by Greeks, hoping for a surprise attack. One of the flanks attacked the Greek military base in Vervena, headed by Kapetan Petros. The Turks tried many times to capture Vervena, but Kapetan Petros and the rest of the Greeks fought gallantly and were able to beat back the Turks. The other two Turkish flanks were also defeated by the Greeks.

By the first week of June, the Greeks were closing in on the fortification of Tripoli, in which they main goal was to lay a siege and capture the city. On June 5, Kapetan Petros with 80 of his men captured a high position from the Turks overlooking Tripoli.

In July 1822, a large Turkish force of 30,000 under the command of Dramalis, entered the Peloponnese in order to reinforce the Turks, who were desperate for help, and to put down the revolution. Realizing this danger, Kolokotronis, as Commander in Chief, ordered Kapetan Petros, the two sons of Kapetan Zaharias, Andreas and Theodoros, and others to go to the fort at Argos and hold back Dramalis and his forces. The strategy here was to try to hold and delay the Turkish force from advancing any further into the Peloponnese, while at the same time, the Greeks would have a chance to round up and organize a large force of their own to battle against Dramalis.

Kapetan Petros entered the fort at Argos around July 10. He had with him about 250 Greeks (most were from the Oinounda region) at Argos ready to fight and defend the fort. Dramalis and his forces arrived on July 12 and he knew that if he advanced any further his rear would be threatened with the enemy holding a strategic position. The Turks attacked the fort, but after ten days, they had nothing to show for it and suffered heavy casualties. Meanwhile, the Greeks at Argos were running out of ammunition and other supplies. To their relief, Kolokotronis had arrived with his force hoping to rescue and pull out the Greeks from the fort. On July 23, Kolokotronis attacked the Turks and were able to beat them back long enough to open a path all the way to the fort and rescue the Greeks. When Kapetan Petros came out of the fort he was hugged and kissed by Kolokotronis who said to him "that there are many individuals with the name Anagnostopoulos, you however should stand out, why not take as your name the famous village that you are from, Barbitsa." He did, and thus from this moment on, he would be know as Petros Anagnostopoulos – Barbitsiotis.

The battle of Argos was a major turning point in the Greek War of Independence. For 11 days, the Greeks under the command of Petros Anagnostopoulos – Barbitsiotis, were able to defend the fort and hold on long enough to be rescued. By delaying Dramalis from advancing, the Greeks in the Peloponnese were able to organize and assemble a large force that was ready to counteract against the Turks. Petros Anagnostopoulos – Barbitsiotis was injured twice in the leg by a gunshot defending the fort, and it is believed that he was the first person to enter the fort and the last to leave.

Shortly thereafter, Barbitsiotis took part in the battle of Corinth against the Turks headed by Dramalis. On July 30, the Greeks arrived just outside of Corinth cutting off all roads and paths. The Turks made a sortie on August 7, but they were badly beaten and had to retreat back to Corinth, leaving behind 60 of their men dead.

During the Greek War of Independence, the Peloponnese formed a council for the purpose of performing and overseeing government duties within Southern Greece. The other purpose was that when the Peloponnese and the other regions in Greece gain their independence from the Ottoman Empire, they would already have a strong foundation for government. Petros Anagnostopoulos – Barbitsiotis was given the responsibility by the "Peloponnese government" to be in charge of and oversee the military arms and supplies for the prefecture of Laconia.

By 1825, as the Geek War of Independence dragged on, the Turks were desperate for help or else everything would be lost. They appointed an Albanian – Turk from Egypt named Ibrahim Pasha as commander of the Turkish - Arab forces in Greece to help put down the revolt and defeat the Greeks. Ibrahim was a young, intelligent, competent, but ruthless commander.

In June 1825, Ibrahim and his forces were passing through Arcadia heading towards the mountain of Tabalas. Kolokotronis was in position waiting for the other Greek forces. The first to arrive was Barbitsiotis and the rest of the Laconian contingent force. Ibrahim decided to attack, but was turned back by the Greeks. The Laconian force decided to counterattack, but they too had no success. The battle lasted all day and continued for a second. The Greeks were heavily outnumbered and in a bad position, decided to pull out from the battlefield and reorganize elsewhere. From this battle, 150 Greeks were killed while the Turks had about 800 dead.

In August 1825, a Turkish force of about two thousand foot soldiers and 600 cavalry, led by an officer named Souliman who was under the command of Ibrahim Pasha, patrolled the area outside of Tripoli when they came across the villages between Silimnas and Davias in Arcadia. They were met by a Greek force, which was separated into three columns. The center and largest column was headed by Barbitsiotis, along with other commanders. In this battle the Turks were defeated and their forces scattered back to Tripoli, while the others retreated to the fort at Davias.

The battles against Ibrahim Pasha continued throughout the Peloponnese. By the end of September 1825, Ibrahim Pasha and his forces had made their way back to Tripoli from Laconia. As he was heading back, the Greeks adopted a guerilla warfare tactic because of the greater number of troops by the enemy. Petros Barbitsiotis attacked the right flank of Pasha's forces near the village of Basara (also known as Vasara) in Laconia, killing 70 in the process. Later on, he took part in the successful siege against the city of Tripoli.

The following year, Ibrahim Pasha was still in the Peloponnese wreaking havoc, slaughtering innocent civilians and burning villages. In July 1826, Ibrahim Pasha decided to once again attack the prefecture of Laconia with a force of about 25 thousand troops. He came across the strategically important city of Mistra, with its high elevation, wanting to capture the fort and control the region. He noticed that the fort was very well defended by Petros Barbitsiotis and two sons of Kapetan Zaharias, Andreas and Sotiro. Since he could not capture the fort, he decided to pull out and head towards another direction, but in the process he lost 22 of his men.

On August 19 1826, a security force belonging to Ibrahim Pasha, consisting of 1,500 men, 300 Greek prisoners and about 12 thousand animals, which included goats, sheep, horses and mules, passed through the village of Basara (Vasara) Laconia. As they were passing through, they were ambushed by a Greek force commanded by Petros Barbitsiotis and other well-known Greek leaders who became heroes of the Greek War of Independence. In the process, the Greeks suffered five casualties, while Pasha's security force had 185 men killed and 17 were taken as prisoners. In addition, the Greeks prisoners were freed from their captors.

In all, Petros Barbitsiotis fought in all of the major battles against the forces of Ibrahim Pasha. He fought for freedom of his people and his land. The danger posed by Ibrahim Pasha was real and not only threatened the termination of the Greek liberation movement, but also putting an end to the Greek race. Barbitsiotis and the other Greeks knew that they had to unite and put up a good fight, or else everything would be lost. After his defeat in Mani, specifically in the battle of Poliaravo on August 28 1826, Ibrahim Pasha retreated back, ending his campaign and never setting foot again in Laconia.

After the military campaigns of Ibrahim Pasha terminated, Petros Barbitsiotis and other Greeks from the Peloponnese crossed over to Central Greece (Roumeli) where they were united with the Greek forces from that region. The commander of the Greek forces in Roumeli was Giorgios Karaiskakis. Petros Barbitsiotis arrived in Central Greece, along with about 1,500 men, in March 1827. He fought alongside Karaiskakis in the battle of Athens, which occurred on April 24, 1827, having about 150 men under his command. In addition, he also took part in the battle of Pireas.

The War of Independence finally came to an end with the Greeks achieving victory and their freedom after nearly four centuries of being under the Turkish yoke. But for Petros Barbitsiotis, there was one more battle that he had to face.

In March of 1832, a group of about 400 bandits from Roumeli, under the leadership of Vaggelis Kontogiannis, crossed over into the Peloponnese, where they began to burn villages, torture and kill innocent victims and rob their money and possessions. During this time he met little or no resistance. They finally reached the prefecture of Laconia, in which one of the first villages they "visited" was the neighboring village of Varvitsa known as

Arachova. He and his men occupied the home of the local priest named Fr. Nikola Leventaki, taking his family and the president of the village Anagnosti Matala as hostages. They demanded money from the villagers and gave them a specific time frame to come up with it.

A few of the men of Kontogiannis, visited Varvitsa where they demanded to see the village president who was none other than Petros Barbitsiotis. They looked down on Barbitsiotis even made fun of him, because he was older, a little frail and that he was limping from the injury to his leg from the battle of Argos. These men made unrealistic demands to Barbitsiotis and threatened that if their demands are not met, they will burn the village and take away the women. Barbitsiotis asked for some time so that he could go tell his co-villagers in order to meet their demands. The bandits agreed and waited for his return in the village-square. But Barbitsiotis told his co-villagers what happened and to take up arms so that they could get rid of these bandits from their village. They surrounded the village-square and told the bandits to leave or they will open fire. The bandits at first were amused and shocked, because they had not met any resistance from any village and they certainly did not expect resistance from a small village like Varvitsa. The villagers from Varvitsa opened fire, and the bandits ran back to Arachova.

That night, Petros Barbitsiotis and the fighting men from the Oinounda region assembled together and went to the Arachova to try to save the village and get rid of these bandits for good. The men who assembled were not only from Varvitsa, but also from Vamvakou, Megali Vrisi, Vresthena, and Basara. They surrounded the area, which was held by the bandits and opened fire. It should be noted that once helped arrived, the villagers from Arachova fought alongside the men from Oinounda. During the battle, the co-leader of the bandits, named Kostas Gidas, was killed. After a few days of fighting the bandits were in a grave position and wanted to negotiate a peaceful settlement. They agreed to return everything they took in Arachova and pay a sum of 30 thousand louphedes as compensation for burning some of the homes in the village.

The song below, which is still sung today, depicts the events described above with the bandits in 1832:

> *A bird flies from the village of Agio Petro.*
> *He sits with those who were slain and looks out*
> *towards Mistra.*
> *And Vaggelis asks (one of his men) Kara-Nikolas:*
> *"Is Arachova far from Agio Petro?"*
> *"Two hours, commander, quickly we shall go.*
> *And if you go to Arachova, be on your best behavior.*
> *Don't tell anyone what we did in the villages of*
> *Doliana and Agio Petro.*
> *There they refer to it as Arachova, and old Varvitsa.*
> *Where they have Petro as commander, Petros*
> *Barbitsiotis.*

Another incident involving Petros Barbitsiotis, which occurred during the 1830's was when Theodoros Kolokotronis decided to pay a visit with his youngest son, Panos. Since he was 15, Kolokotronis frequently visited Varvitsa to see Kapetan Zaharias, or in his later life, Petros Barbitsiotis. Apparently, during this particular visit, he slept overnight in the house of Barbitsiotis. The next morning, Barbitsiotis asked him if he had a good night sleep. Kolokotronis replied he did, except for the fact that there were some gnats biting him during the night. To which, Barbitsiotis took his family, Kolokotronis and his son out of his residence, only to burn his own house!

In 1844, Petros Barbitsiotis was elected to the Greek Parlament, representing the Mistra area. He played an influential role in pursuing his co-villagers to take up land and residence in the village of Skoura. After the Greek War of Independence, many villagers from Varvitsa took up residence in Skoura, thus having a dual residency. In the winter they would live in Skoura, while in the summer, they would stay in the cool surroundings of Varvitsa. Petros Barbitsiotis lived a long and active life. He died on April 3 1871, at the age of 86.

Petros Anagnostopoulos – Barbitsiotis played a major role in the Greek War of Independence by participating in almost all of the major battles in the Peloponnese and beyond. He was an intelligent commander and a brave fighter who was unselfish and didn't care about his own personal interests. He would always help out in any way he could for the cause of liberation. What was always on his mind was the freedom of Greece and the good for the people. He was in charge of the Eastern Laconian forces, and in the process, was twice injured in the leg at Argos, but that never stopped him from fighting for freedom. Petros Anagnostopoulos – Barbitsiotis was a true patriot. "Bronze chested", as he was always known as, changed his name to Barbitsiotis, under the request by Kolokotronis, to honor the famous village he came from. He truly showed everyone what it means to be from Varvitsa, and gave pride and honor to his home village and to Kapetan Zaharias, the man who taught him.

Kapetan Petros Anagnostopoulos - Barbitsiotis

CHAPTER FIVE

This chapter will cover the two very famous villages of Laconia, Varvitsa and Logastra. Since this book is about the history of Zaharias, Nikolopoulos and Barbitsiotis, it is necessary to mention about the villages they came from. Also the fact that these villages are brought up so many times throughout the book, it is only fitting that some information be provided. It should be noted that Zaharias also lived in Skoufomiti, located in the Mani region, for a good number of years and that information about this village has already been covered in chapter two of this book.

The village of Varvitsa is also known as Barbitsa, which was the more common reference prior and during the Greek War of Independence. The reason for this is that when the Venetians took control of the Peloponnese during the late 1600's, they conducted many studies, geographical surveys and population census. As they were doing this, many of the villages they came across, which began with a "v" sound they made it into a "B" sound. And the reason for this is that the Greek alphabet "B" has a "v" sound to it. But to the Venetians, they saw the Greek alphabet "B" as a Latin letter, so therefore they would pronounce it with a "b" sound, hence Barbitsa. Other neighboring villages were also treated the same way, such as Vamvakou was Bambakou, Vresthena became Bresthena, and Vassara was known as Bassara.

Varvitsa is found on the western side of Mt. Parnon, near the peak, and its elevation is about 1,060 meters above sea level. It is near the Laconian-Arcadian border and is about 43 kilometers from the city of Sparta. Just a stone throw away to the northeast is the peak of the mountain, which is about 1,935 meters above sea level. It has plenty of clean air, cool climate even in the summer and clean and cool water with a panoramic breathtaking view of the countryside. The favorite past time here is sheep and goat herding.

There are two prevailing theories as to how the name of the village, Varvitsa, came about. The first theory mentions that the name comes from another village called Vervitsa, located in the Gortynia region of Arcadia, in which some of the early family settlers of Varvitsa were from. The other theory is that the name is of Slavic origin, dating back to the period when the Slavs made their way and settled within the various parts of the Peloponnese. The word Varvitsa in Slavic means certain small trees, which flourish near streams of water. Back in the early days, Varvitsa was known to have this in the land around them.

Fotiou Chysanthopoulos, also known as Photakos, lived and fought during the Greek War of Independence and later on in his life, wrote his memoirs about the war and on other items. In his book titled "Bioi Peloponnesion Andron" (Biography of Peloponnesian Men, 1996 first published in 1888 Athens, Greece publisher Vergina) on page 66, he mentions that Varvitsa is famous because it was the birthplace of the well-known hero Kapetan Zaharias. But there was another hero who was born in Varvitsa and played a significant role in liberating Greece and that was Petros Anagnostopoulos-Barbitsiotis.

The village of Varvitsa was first settled between 1650-1680. The original settlers had mainly come from the various parts of Laconia, Mani and Arcadia. These settlers were actually klephtic rebels and their families, who were being sought after by the Turks, and were jumping around from place to place in order to find a secured and safe area to get away from the threat or danger. Prior to settling in Varvitsa, these klephtes had their living quarters to the west in an area known as Kalyvia. But after a short time, they decided to relocate southwest of the village, which is an area known as Ai-Thanasi. This particular area is further up Mt. Parnon, and even today a few ruins of old homes and a church can still be found. Eventually, they left Ai-Thanasi and decided to finally settle a little further down, into what would become known as Varvitsa.

When they first settled in Varvitsa, the original habitants found an abundance of water and a deep thick forest around them. Varvitsa was ideal for protection and offered a natural defense barrier against any enemy attacks. With the forest and the high elevation, which can be used to lookout for an approaching enemy, the settlers had a significant advantage.

The settlers of Varvitsa built their homes, and in the middle of the village, they built a small church named Agios Demetrios. By 1715, as the population of Varvitsa started to increase, the church of Agios Demetrios expanded to accommodate the enlarged congregation.

The village of Logastra can be found in the eastern side of Mount Taygetos, located in the northern part of Laconia. With its beautiful surroundings and breathtaking view of the countryside, the village has an elevation of about 600 meters above sea level. It has plenty of water and natural springs, which flows down to the Evrotas River. At the peak of the village, there is a small church named Agiou Nikolaou.

It is believed that Logastra was first settled between 1100-1200 AD by Byzantine Greeks, at the height of the Byzantine Empire. Throughout the years, there were many foreign invaders who came down and swept through the Peloponnese, in which many settled in different parts of the region. One of the largest ethnic groups to have settled in the Peloponnese were the Slavs. Because of this many Greeks were driven away from their homes, along the coast and the valleys, for the safer grounds of the mountains. Mount Taygetos was no exception, in which many Greeks made their way near the peek of Logastra, to an area known as Kerasovas.

The name Logastra is derived from the fact that the village and the surrounding area has always been known for it's very thick forest. This not only offered protection for the village, but also an abundance supply of wood. Logastra has a natural beauty and is an outdoor lover's paradise. It has its share of churches, with the largest being that of Agioi Taxarchas.

Logastra is where the Nikolopoulos family was based at and they were a strong clan, which controlled not only the surrounding area, but also the northern part of Laconia for many decades. They set up a military training base for the main purpose of uniting and teaching the Greek rebels the art of guerilla warfare. Many well-known and heroic individuals passed through Logastra and "the base of Nikolopoulos" for many different reasons. One of those heroic individuals was Kapetan Zaharias, who first went to Logastra after he decided to become a rebel fighter. So many future leaders of the Greek War of Independence visited and were influenced by Logastra, that it was at one point referred to as "Kapetanochori," meaning village of Kapetans. Logastra and Varvitsa had the most influential and first military bases probably in the Peloponnese, if not then certainly within Laconia, which was used to prepare for the resistance and to fight against tyranny and the occupation by the Ottoman Empire.

As mentioned, the villages of Varvitsa and Logastra are famous because of the fact that Kapetan Zaharias, Petros Anagnostopoulos-Barbitsiotis and Andonis Nikolopoulos all came from there and became heroes of Modern Greece. They were heroes because they paved the road for Greek independence, they fought in the war for Greek liberation and they died for Greece, they died for freedom. Many songs and ballads were written and sung back in the days before and after the Greek War of Independence. Amazingly, most of these songs are still sung today and are classified as either Greek klephtic songs, or Greek folk songs. The following song describes a particular battle, in which all three heroes, Zaharias, Nikolopoulos and Barbitsiotis are mentioned. It is still sung today in many parts of the Southern Peloponnese:

> *Rifles shooting at the forts of Varvitsa.*
> *Zaharias was feasting, the commander of klephtes.*
> *Along with old Andonis (Nikolopoulos), Yiannias, Gioros and Bobolas,*
> *The flagbearer Yiannios (Bouloukos) and Petros Barbitsiotis.*
> *Yiousouf Agas was very upset when he heard about the feast.*
> *He sends a messenger to Varvitsa.*
> *"What is going on here, Kapetans;*
> *We were sent here by Yiousouf Agas, in order for you to submit to him!"*
> *"What are you saying you Mourtatides and old-Albanians;*
> *When have you ever seen klephtes to submit to the pashas.*
> *Go back to the Kotsabasides, go back to the Turks*
> *And never set foot here again, never come back.*
> *Here is the famous Varvitsa, which is full of klephtes,*
> *We talk with our weapons, our bullets and gunpowder."*

Village of Varvitsa (Barbitsa)

Village of Logastra with Mt. Taygetos in the backdrop

CHAPTER SIX

Many bona fide heroes came out of the Greek War of Independence and some died fighting for freedom. But the Greek War of Independence never would of come about if it wasn't for the heroes who came before it and paved the way for liberation. These heroes laid the foundation for the freedom of Greece from the Turkish yoke. Without a foundation, or even a strong foundation for that matter, any hopes or motion for independence would collapse like a deck of cards. The three heroes mentioned in this book either laid the foundation for liberation, or were involved in some outcome, which kept the hopes alive for independence. Zaharias united all the klephtic rebels for the purpose of starting a revolution. Nikolopoulos fought his entire life for freedom and when he died fighting in Vlachokerasia, it stirred up the other Greeks to join and fight in the war for independence. Barbitsiotis not only fought in every major battle in the Peloponnese, but was also present at the battle of Acropolis, the symbol of Hellenism, and fought at the battle of Argos, which was a major turning point in the war for liberation. It should be noted that there were other heroes and individuals before the Greek War of Independence who also played a major role in Greek affairs and paved the way for freedom.

Zaharias, Nikolopoulos and Barbitsiotis played a major role not only in their home region of Laconia, but also played a significant role in the Peloponnese and Greece. They changed the history of Modern Greece by planning for and fighting in the war for independence. What makes it even more interesting is the close association and ties between the three heroes. Zaharias went from Varvitsa to Logastra to become a klepht. After a few years he married a relative of the Nikolopoulos family. The two families had a very close bond, in that they supported each other and would go on to fight Turkish oppression. Also, one of the daughters of Zaharias married the son of Andonis Nikolopoulos, named Nikolas. The association to be made with Petros Anagnostopoulos-Barbitsiotis is the fact that he was taught, from a very early age, by Zaharias and that he tried to come to the rescue of Andonis Nikolopoulos in the battle of Vlachokerasia.

While there have been a good number of history books that have mentioned about the accomplishments and heroism of Zaharias, Nikolopoulos and Barbitsiotis, more is still needed. Also, these three heroes still have not received the recognition and honor they rightfully deserve. There needs to be a greater respect, not only by the people, but also by the governments, for the three heroes who accomplished so much and sacrificed their lives. The schools and universities should teach and educate the students about their history, so that they never forget and that they realize what these heroes did. Greek societies, organizations, communities and even the Greek governments, should pay tribute and honor these heroes, which would keep their memories alive. Finally, in 1998 the city of Sparta unveiled the statue of Kapetan Zaharias, why not also have other statues erected of Zaharias in Varvitsa and Skoufomiti. In addition, statues should also be erected for Andonis Nikolopoulos, and Petros Barbitsiotis. I hope this becomes a reality sooner rather than later.

The following three poems, written by me, are about Zaharias, Nikolopoulos and Barbitsiotis. The first poem is dedicated to Kapetan Zaharias and it was first written in Greek, but here it has been translated into English. The poem is titled "Zaharias the Great."

O Zaharias from Varvitsa he came.
And to the Turkish Pashas he never submitted.
He would always be taking care of the klephtes and
the poor.
O Zaharias he would chase after the Turks.
With his fierce sword he will eat them.
Since this is how he fights.
He became Commander in Chief of the Peloponnese.
With the purpose of gaining freedom.
And united and strengthened the klephtic rebels.
He goes to the famous Mani region.
And he does battle in Dafni.
Zaharias never loses a battle.
Zaharias builds forts in Skoufomiti.
He captures the Turks and Napoleon sends him
military supplies in Kardamili.
This is Kapetan Zaharias.
This is Commander in Chief Zaharias.
This is Zaharias the Great.

The second poem, titled "Nikolopoulos," is dedicated to Andonis
Nikolopoulos. Here then is the poem:

The sun rises from the east.
Fast approaching Vlachokerasia are the Turks.
It's Easter morning and the Greeks are preparing for
a
feast.
They cry out "Christ has risen, he has truly risen.

And Greece shall be reborn and rise up again."
Nikolopoulos prepares for battle, the Turks he will
fight and defeat.
With his three hundred men, he orders to attack.
He stands his ground he has no desire to retreat.

With all seemed lost, he takes out his sword and
charges at the Turks.
As he charged, he kills the Turkish commander.
But in the end the hero, Nikolopoulos, fell in battle.
His death brought on a new life.
It gave new life to the Greeks fighting for freedom.

The third and final poem titled "Barbitsiotis," is dedicated to
another great hero from Varvitsa, Petros Anagnostopoulos-
Barbitsiotis. The poem is as follows:

O Petros Barbitsiotis see how he fights.
From Varvitsa to Vervaina.
From Argos to the Acropolis.
He takes out his sword and charges at the vastly
numerous Turks.
One by one the Turks are being slaughtered.
So much blood is spilled that it flows down like a river
from a mountain.

BIBLIOGRAPHY

The bibliographical sources for this book are almost all in Greek. The authors and titles of the Greek sources have been translated into English text.

Alexander, John C. *Brigandage and Public Order in the Morea 1685-1806.* Athens, 1985.

Antonopoulos, G. *Viographia tou Zaharia. Dragatsanion,* July 1888.

Chysanthopoulos, Photios (Photakos). *Apomnimonevmata peri tis Ellinikis epanastaseos.* 4 vols. Athens, 1955.
          Vioi Peloponnesion Andron. Athens, 1888.

Doukas, Panagiotis. *H Sparti dia mesou ton aionon.* New York, 1922.

Kandeloros, Takes, Ch. *O armatolismos tis Peloponnesou, 1500-1821.* Athens, 1924.

Kargakos, Sarantos. *Zaharias Barbitsiotis. O daskalos tis klephtourias.* Athens, 1998.

Kolokotronis, Theodoros. *Apomnimonevmata (G. Tertseti).* Ed. Tasos Vournas. Athens, 1977.

Kontakis, Anagnostes. *Apomnimonevmata.* Vol. XI, pp. 5-84 from the series of *Apomnimonevmata ton Agoniston tou 21.* E.G. Protopsaltes. 20 vols. Athens, 1956-57.

Kostara, Nikos I. *O Zaharias Barbitsiotis. O threilikos klephtokoursaros tou Moria. Naftiki Ellas,* August 1995.

Leake, William Martin. *Travels in the Morea.* 3 vols. London, 1830.

Matheos, Nikos D. *O protoklephtes Zaharias h epohe tou kai to 21.* Athens, 1998.

Philemon, Yiannis. *Dokimon istorikon peri tis Ellinikis*

epanastaseos. 4 vols. Athens, 1859-1861 *Dokimon istorikon peri tis Philikis Etairias.* Nafplion, 1834.

Phrantzis, Amvrosios. *Epitome istorias tis anagennitheisis Ellados archomeni apo tou etous 1715 kai ligousa to 1835.* 4 vols. Athens, 1839-1841.

Roumeliotis, Potis G. *H Barbitsa kai h Skoura Lakedaimonos.* Athens, 1983.

Sheridan, Charles Brinsley. *Popular songs of Greece.* London, 1825 translated from the book Fauriel, C.C. *Chants populaires de la Grece moderne.* Paris, 1824.

Trikoupes, Spyridon. *Istoria tis Ellinikis epanastaseos.* 4 vols. Athens, 1860-1862.

Vlachogiannes, Yiannis. *Klephtes tou Moria 1715-1820.* Athens, 1935.

Yiannakopoulou, Eleni. *Metaxi Gallon kai Agglon: Mia alli opsi tou perigitismou kai tis deisdisis ton xenon sti Mani (1780-1807).* pp. 227-272 from the book *Mani: Marturies gia to choro kai ti koinonia. Perigites kai epistimonikes apostoles (15th – 19th century).* Areopoli, 1993.

Zannetos, Philios. *Zaharias Barbitsiotis, 1759-1805. Laconika I* (1932), pp. 83-166.